GCSE OCR 21st Century

Combined Science

There are only three ways to make sure you're fully prepared for the GCSE Combined Science exams — practice, practice and practice.

That's why we've packed this brilliant CGP book with realistic exam-style questions for every topic, and we've got all the practicals covered too.

And since you'll be tested on a wide range of topics in the real exams, we've also included sections of mixed questions for Biology, Chemistry and Physics!

Exam Practice Workbook
Foundation Level

Contents

✓ Use the tick boxes to check off the topics you've completed.

How to Use This Book...1

Chapter B1 — You and Your Genes

Cells and Genetic Material..2
Cells and Microscopes..3
DNA and Characteristics..4
Genetic Diagrams..5
More Genetic Diagrams..6
Genome Research and Testing..7
Genetic Engineering...8

Chapter B2 — Keeping Healthy

Health and Disease...9
How Disease Spreads..10
Defending Against Pathogens...12
The Human Immune System...13
Reducing and Preventing the Spread of Disease............14
Vaccinations..16
Culturing Microorganisms...17
Non-Communicable Diseases...19
Interpreting Data on Disease...21
Investigating Pulse Rate..22
Treating Disease..23
Treating Cardiovascular Disease..24
Developing New Medicines..25

Chapter B3 — Living Together — Food and Ecosystems

Enzymes..26
Photosynthesis...28
Investigating Photosynthesis..29
Investigating the Rate of Photosynthesis.........................30
Diffusion, Osmosis and Active Transport..........................31
Transport in Plants and Prokaryotes...................................32
Investigating Diffusion and Osmosis...................................33
Xylem and Phloem..35
Stomata...36
Transpiration Rate...37
Using a Potometer..38
Ecosystems and Interactions Between Organisms.......39
Abiotic Factors and Investigating Distribution................40
Investigating Ecosystems..41
More on Investigating Ecosystems.....................................42
Investigating Factors Affecting Distribution....................43
Food Chains and Food Webs..44

Making and Breaking Biological Molecules......................45
Testing for Biological Molecules..46
Cycles in Ecosystems...47
More on Cycles in Ecosystems...48

Chapter B4 — Using Food and Controlling Growth

Respiration...49
More on Respiration...50
The Cell Cycle and Mitosis...51
Microscopy...52
More Microscopy...53
Sexual Reproduction and Meiosis.......................................54
Stem Cells..55

Chapter B5 — The Human Body — Staying Alive

Exchange of Materials...56
Human Exchange Surfaces..57
The Circulatory System...58
Blood Vessels..59
Blood..60
The Nervous System..61
Reflexes...62
Hormones in Reproduction..63
Contraception...64
Homeostasis and Blood Sugar Level..................................65

Chapter B6 — Life on Earth — Past, Present and Future

Natural Selection and Evolution..66
Evidence for Evolution..67
Selective Breeding..68
Classification...69
Biodiversity..70
Maintaining Biodiversity..72

Chapter C1 — Air and Water

States of Matter...73
Changing State...74
Chemical Formulas..75
Chemical Equations..76
Endothermic and Exothermic Reactions...........................77
Bond Energies...78
The Evolution of the Atmosphere.......................................79

Combustion and Greenhouse Gases 80
Climate Change 81
Reducing Greenhouse Gas Emissions 82
Pollutants and Tests for Gases 83
Water Treatment 84

Chapter C2 — Chemical Patterns
The History of the Atom 86
The Atom 87
Atoms and Isotopes 88
The Periodic Table 89
Electronic Structure 90
Metals and Non-Metals 91
Group 1 Elements and Their Reactions 92
Group 7 Elements and Their Reactions 95
Group 0 Elements 97
Ions 98
Ionic Bonding 99
Ionic Compounds 100

Chapter C3 — Chemicals of the Natural Environment
Metallic Bonding 101
Reactivity and Reactions of Metals 102
More Reactions of Metals 103
Extracting Metals 104
Electrolysis 105
Covalent Bonding 107
Simple Covalent Substances 108
Empirical Formulas 109
Homologous Series and Alkanes 110
Fractional Distillation of Crude Oil 111
Uses of Crude Oil 112

Chapter C4 — Material Choices
Polymers 113
Giant Covalent Structures 114
Bulk Properties of Materials 115
Types of Materials and Their Uses 116
Reuse and Recycling 118
Life Cycle Assessments 119
Nanoparticles and Their Uses 120

Chapter C5 — Chemical Analysis
Purity and Mixtures 122
Chromatography 123
Interpreting Chromatograms 124
Distillation 125
Separating Mixtures 126

Relative Mass 127
Conservation of Mass 128
Acids, Alkalis and Standard Solutions 130
Titrations 131
Evaluating Titration Data 132

Chapter C6 — Making Useful Chemicals
Acids, Alkalis and pH 133
Reactions of Acids 134
Making Salts 135
Rates of Reactions 137
Reaction Rates and Catalysts 138
Measuring Reaction Rates 139
Finding Reaction Rates from Graphs 140
Using Tangents to Find Reaction Rates 141
Dynamic Equilibrium 142

Chapter P1 — Radiation and Waves
Wave Basics 143
Wave Speed 144
Wave Experiments 145
Reflection 146
Refraction 147
Investigating Refraction 148
The Electromagnetic Spectrum 149
Energy Levels in Atoms 150
Uses of EM Radiation 151
More Uses of EM Radiation 152
Temperature and Radiation 153

Chapter P2 — Sustainable Energy
Energy Stores and Conservation of Energy 154
Energy Transfers 155
Efficiency and Power 156
Reducing Unwanted Energy Transfers 157
Energy Resources 158
Renewable Energy Resources 159
Trends in Energy Use 161
The National Grid 162

Chapter P3 — Electric Circuits
Current, Potential Difference and Resistance 163
Describing and Drawing Circuits 164
Investigating Resistance 165
LDRs and Thermistors 166
I-V Characteristics 167
Circuit Devices and I-V Characteristics 168
Energy in Circuits 169

Series Circuits 170
Parallel Circuits 171
Investigating Series and Parallel Circuits 172
Electrical Power 173
Transformers 174
Permanent and Induced Magnets 175
Magnetism and Electromagnetism 176
Solenoids and Electromagnets 177

Chapter P4 — Explaining Motion

Forces and Newton's Third Law 178
Mass and Weight 179
Distance, Displacement, Speed and Velocity 180
Measuring and Converting Units 181
Acceleration 182
Investigating Motion 183
Distance-Time Graphs 184
Velocity-Time Graphs 185
Free Body Diagrams and Resultant Forces 186
Newton's First and Second Laws 187
Reaction Times 188
Stopping Distances 189
Vehicle Safety 190
Work Done and Power 191
Kinetic and Potential Energy Stores 192
Describing Energy Transfers 193

Chapter P5 — Radioactive Materials

The History of the Atom 194
The Modern Model of the Atom 195
Isotopes and Radioactive Decay 196
Nuclear Equations 197
Activity and Half-life 198
Dangers of Radioactivity 199
More on the Dangers of Radioactivity 200
Uses of Radiation 201

Chapter P6 — Matter — Models and Explanations

Density 202
The Particle Model 203
More on the Particle Model 204
Specific Heat Capacity 205
Specific Latent Heat 206
Heating and Doing Work 207
Forces and Elasticity 208
Investigating Elasticity 209

Mixed Questions

Biology Mixed Questions 210
Chemistry Mixed Questions 216
Physics Mixed Questions 223

Published by CGP

Editors: Alex Billings, Mary Falkner, Robin Flello, Emily Forsberg, Emily Garrett, Emily Howe, Duncan Lindsay, Rachael Rogers, Frances Rooney, Hayley Thompson and Sarah Williams.

Contributors: Ian Davis, Mark Edwards, Chris Workman.

ISBN: 978 1 78294 509 3

With thanks to Phil Armstrong, Matthew Benyohai, Ciara McGlade, Glenn Rogers, Jamie Sinclair and Karen Wells for the proofreading.

With thanks to Jan Greenway for the copyright research.

The graph on page 21 showing the incidence rate of lung cancer in men between 1990 and 2000 is from Cancer Research UK, http://www.cancerresearchuk.org/health-professional/lung-cancer-incidence-statistics#heading-Two, accessed in February 2016.

With thanks to iStock.com for permission to use the image on page 52.

Data used to construct the graph on page 81 provided by the European Environment Agency.

Clipart from Corel®
Illustrations by: Sandy Gardner Artist, email sandy@sandygardner.co.uk
Printed by Elanders Ltd, Newcastle upon Tyne.

Based on the classic CGP style created by Richard Parsons.

Text, design, layout and original illustrations © Coordination Group Publications Ltd. (CGP) 2016.
All rights reserved.

Photocopying this book is not permitted. Extra copies are available from CGP with next day delivery.
0800 1712 712 • www.cgpbooks.co.uk

1

How to Use This Book

- Hold the book upright, approximately 50 cm from your face, ensuring that the text looks like this, not sıɥʇ.
- In case of emergency, press the two halves of the book together firmly in order to close.
- Before attempting to use this book, read the following safety information:

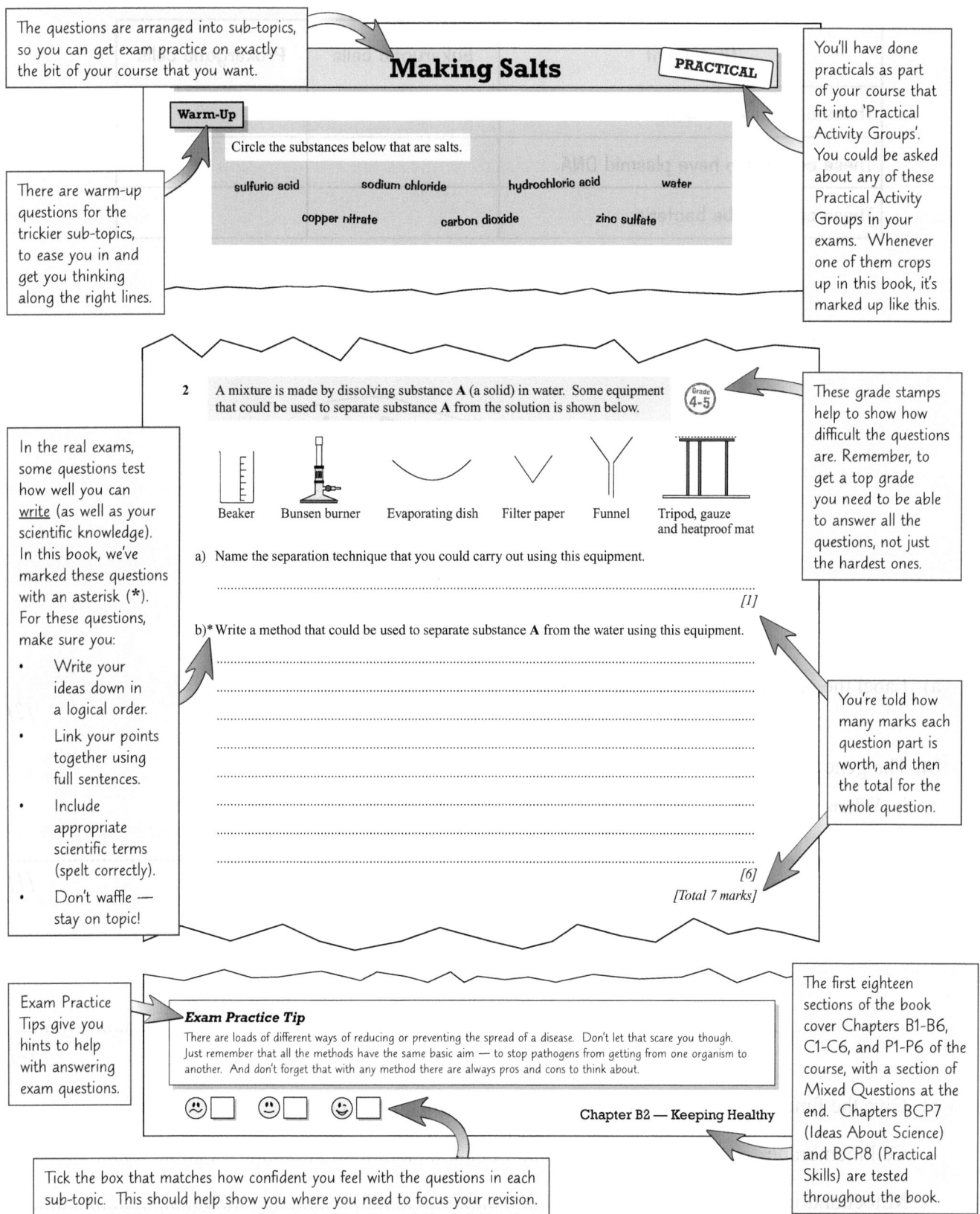

The questions are arranged into sub-topics, so you can get exam practice on exactly the bit of your course that you want.

You'll have done practicals as part of your course that fit into 'Practical Activity Groups'. You could be asked about any of these Practical Activity Groups in your exams. Whenever one of them crops up in this book, it's marked up like this.

There are warm-up questions for the trickier sub-topics, to ease you in and get you thinking along the right lines.

These grade stamps help to show how difficult the questions are. Remember, to get a top grade you need to be able to answer all the questions, not just the hardest ones.

In the real exams, some questions test how well you can write (as well as your scientific knowledge). In this book, we've marked these questions with an asterisk (*). For these questions, make sure you:
- Write your ideas down in a logical order.
- Link your points together using full sentences.
- Include appropriate scientific terms (spelt correctly).
- Don't waffle — stay on topic!

You're told how many marks each question part is worth, and then the total for the whole question.

Exam Practice Tips give you hints to help with answering exam questions.

The first eighteen sections of the book cover Chapters B1-B6, C1-C6, and P1-P6 of the course, with a section of Mixed Questions at the end. Chapters BCP7 (Ideas About Science) and BCP8 (Practical Skills) are tested throughout the book.

Tick the box that matches how confident you feel with the questions in each sub-topic. This should help show you where you need to focus your revision.

- There's also a Physics Equations List at the back of this book — you'll be given these equations in your exam. You can look up equations on this list to help you answer some of the physics questions in this book.

Chapter B1 — You and Your Genes

Cells and Genetic Material

Warm-Up

Complete the table to show whether each statement is **true** for eukaryotic cells or prokaryotic cells. Tick **one** box in each row.

Statement	Eukaryotic cells	Prokaryotic cells
These cells have a nucleus.		
These cells often have plasmid DNA.		
These cells can be bacteria.		

1   The diagram below shows an animal cell.

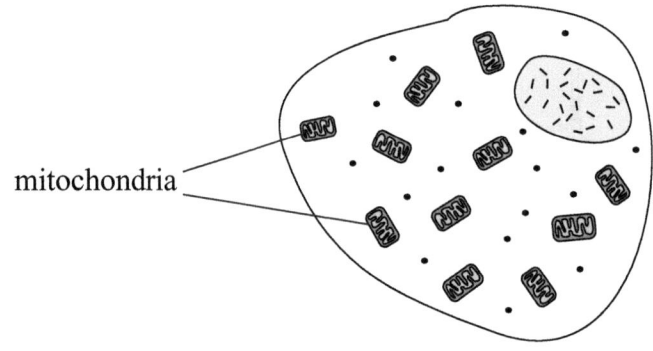

mitochondria

a) Label the cell membrane and the nucleus on the diagram above.

[2]

b) The genetic material in the cell above is located in the nucleus.

i) Where is the genetic material located in a prokaryotic cell?

....
[1]

ii) Describe the function of the genetic material in a cell.

....

....
[2]

c) Give the function of each of the following parts of an animal cell:

Cell membrane ....

Mitochondria ....
[2]

[Total 7 marks]

Cells and Microscopes   PRACTICAL

1 A student wants to use a light microscope to view a sample of onion cells. *Grade 3-4*

a) The student adds a drop of iodine stain to her sample.
Which statement best describes why a stain might be used to view a sample of tissue?
Place a tick (✓) in the box next to the correct answer.

To make the specimen easier to cut. ☐

To make the specimen easier to see. ☐

To prevent air bubbles forming. ☐

To help the cover slip stick to the slide. ☐

[1]

The diagram on the right shows the light microscope that the student plans to use. Three different objective lenses are labelled on the diagram with their magnification.

b) The student begins by selecting the lowest-powered objective lens. State the magnification of this lens.

....
[1]

After she has selected the objective lens, the student looks down the eyepiece and uses the adjustment knobs.

c) Label the eyepiece and **one** of the adjustment knobs on the diagram.

[2]

d) What is the purpose of the adjustment knobs?
Place a tick (✓) in the box next to the correct answer.

To increase the brightness of the lamp. ☐

To increase the size of the image. ☐

To move the stage so that the image is brought into focus. ☐

To change the position of the slide on the stage. ☐

[1]

e) The student produces a scientific drawing of the onion cells. Her drawing is shown below.

Give **two** ways in which the student could improve her drawing.

1. ....

2. ....

[2]

[Total 7 marks]

Chapter B1 — You and Your Genes

DNA and Characteristics

1 Draw **one** line from each word on the left to its definition on the right. The first one has been done for you.

Word   **Definition**

genetic variant — A different version of a gene.

nucleotide

gene

chromosome

A long molecule of coiled DNA.

A section of DNA that codes for a protein.

A single monomer in a DNA polymer.

[Total 2 marks]

2 Organisms have many different genes.

a) What term is used to describe the entire genetic material of an organism?

....

[1]

b) Explain how genes affect what an organism looks like.

....

....

....

[3]

[Total 4 marks]

3 Helen and Stephanie are identical twins. This means they have identical DNA.

a) Helen and Stephanie both have a red hair phenotype. What is meant by the term 'phenotype'?

....

[1]

b) Helen weighs 7 kg more than Stephanie.
Explain whether this is due to genes, environmental factors or both.

....

....

[2]

[Total 3 marks]

Exam Practice Tip

It's hard to get the right answer if you don't know what the question's asking you — so make sure you learn all the scientific words related to this topic (genome, phenotype, etc.). You could also be asked to define them in the exam.

Chapter B1 — You and Your Genes

Genetic Diagrams

Warm-Up

Draw lines to match each word on the left to its correct definition on the right.

heterozygous   Having two alleles the same for a particular gene.

homozygous   Having two different alleles for a particular gene.

1   Hair length in dogs is controlled by two alleles. Short hair is caused by the dominant allele, 'H'. Long hair is caused by the recessive allele, 'h'.

The incomplete Punnett square on the right shows a cross between a short-haired dog and a long-haired dog.

a) State the genotype of the long-haired parent in this cross.

....
[1]

b) Complete the Punnett square to show the possible genotypes of the dogs' offspring.
[1]
[Total 2 marks]

2   Height in pea plants is controlled by a single gene. The allele for tall plants (T) is dominant over the allele for dwarf plants (t).

A student says that a pea plant must have the genotype TT to be tall. Is the student correct? Explain your answer.

....

....
[Total 2 marks]

3   Cystic fibrosis is an inherited disorder. The allele which causes cystic fibrosis is a recessive allele, 'f'. 'F' represents the dominant allele.

An incomplete genetic diagram is shown on the right. It shows the possible inheritance of cystic fibrosis from one couple.

a) Complete the genetic diagram to show the missing gametes' genotypes and the missing offspring's genotype.
[2]

b) What proportion of the possible offspring are heterozygous?

....
[1]

c) What proportion of the possible offspring have cystic fibrosis?

....
[1]
[Total 4 marks]

Chapter B1 — You and Your Genes

More Genetic Diagrams

1 The diagram below shows a family tree.
The family have a history of an inherited disorder.

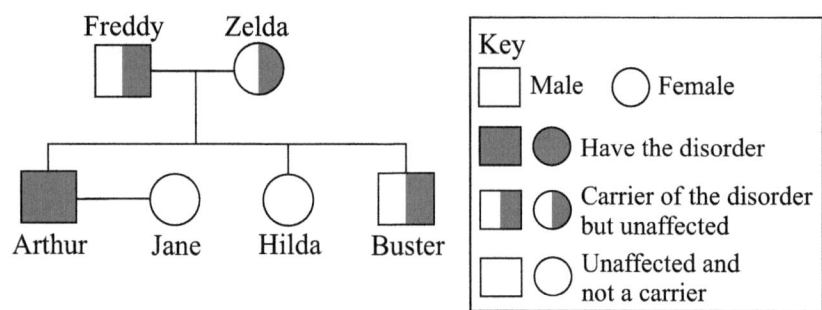

a) Name the child of Freddy and Zelda who is unaffected by the disorder and not a carrier.

....
[1]

The disorder is caused by a recessive allele, 'd'. The dominant allele is 'D'.

b) What is **Arthur's** genotype?
Place a tick (✓) in the box next to the correct answer.

DD ☐   Dd ☐   dd ☐   d ☐
[1]

c) What is **Zelda's** genotype?

....
[1]

[Total 3 marks]

2 The diagram below shows how the biological sex of offspring is determined.

a) Complete the diagram to show the sex chromosomes of the gametes and the offspring.
[1]

b) Give the ratio of male to female offspring. ....
[1]

[Total 2 marks]

Genome Research and Testing

1 In the future, genetic testing could allow doctors to determine which drugs will work best for their patients. What is the term for this kind of treatment? Place a tick (✓) in the box next to the correct answer.

family planning ☐

genetic modification ☐

personalised medicine ☐

genetic engineering ☐

[Total 1 mark]

2 During some fertility treatments, embryos are created in the laboratory. These embryos can be tested for genetic disorders, such cystic fibrosis, before being implanted into the womb. There are lots of arguments for and against the genetic testing of embryos.

a) Give **one** argument **against** the genetic testing of embryos.

....

....
[1]

b) Give **one** argument **for** the genetic testing of embryos.

....

....
[1]

A woman who has not undergone fertility treatment is pregnant.

c) Describe **one** way in which doctors may be able to determine whether or not her unborn child will have cystic fibrosis, while the child is still in the womb.

....

....

....
[2]
[Total 4 marks]

Exam Practice Tip
Many people think that genome research is great news for the world of medicine. But, as with lots of new developments in science, there are some possible downsides to consider too. Make sure you're aware of both the pros and the cons because you might have to write about both sides of the argument in an exam question. You lucky thing.

Chapter B1 — You and Your Genes

Genetic Engineering

1 Crop plants can be genetically engineered to be resistant to herbicides.

a) Describe what is meant by genetic engineering.

....

....
[2]

b) What is the benefit of genetically engineering crop plants to be resistant to herbicides?
Place a tick (✓) in the box next to the correct answer.

It makes the crop healthier. ☐   It can increase crop yield. ☐

It makes the crop cheaper to buy. ☐   It reduces damage to the crop from pests. ☐
[1]

[Total 3 marks]

2 Some people have concerns about the use of genetic engineering.

a) Suggest **one** concern that someone may have about the use of genetic engineering in animals.

....

....
[1]

b) Suggest **one** concern that someone may have about the use of genetic engineering in crops.

....

....
[1]

[Total 2 marks]

3 Some scientists are investigating the number of wild flowers in two meadows. One meadow is next to a field containing a genetically modified (GM) crop. The other meadow is next to a field containing a non-GM crop. The scientists compare their results for the two meadows.

a) Suggest why the scientists are carrying out this investigation.

....

....
[1]

b) Suggest **one** thing the scientists could do to make their results more valid.

....
[1]

[Total 2 marks]

Chapter B1 — You and Your Genes

Chapter B2 — Keeping Healthy

Health and Disease

Warm-Up

What is a pathogen? Circle the correct answer.

- A type of disease.
- A microorganism that causes disease.
- Something used to treat a disease.
- Something used to prevent the spread of disease.

1 Diseases can be communicable or non-communicable.

a) What is the difference between a communicable disease and a non-communicable disease? Place a tick (✓) in the box next to the correct answer.

- Only communicable diseases can cause symptoms. ☐
- Only communicable diseases can spread between people. ☐
- Only non-communicable diseases can spread between people. ☐
- Only communicable diseases are linked to unhealthy lifestyles. ☐

[1]

b) Which of the following is the cause of **communicable** diseases? Place a tick (✓) in the box next to the correct answer.

smoking ☐   pathogens ☐   obesity ☐   trauma ☐

[1]

[Total 2 marks]

2 Communicable diseases can often be identified by the symptoms that they cause.

a) Give **two** ways in which diseases can cause symptoms in an organism.

1. ....
2. ....

[2]

b) Explain why the symptoms of a communicable disease may not appear immediately after the person gets the disease.

....
....

[1]

[Total 3 marks]

Exam Practice Tip

Make sure that you understand the differences between communicable and non-communicable diseases — you might be given information on a disease you don't know about in the exam and asked to work out which category it fits into.

How Disease Spreads

1 Many human diseases are caused by pathogens.

Draw lines to match each **human disease** to the **type of pathogen** that causes it and the **method** by which that pathogen spreads. The first two lines have been done for you.

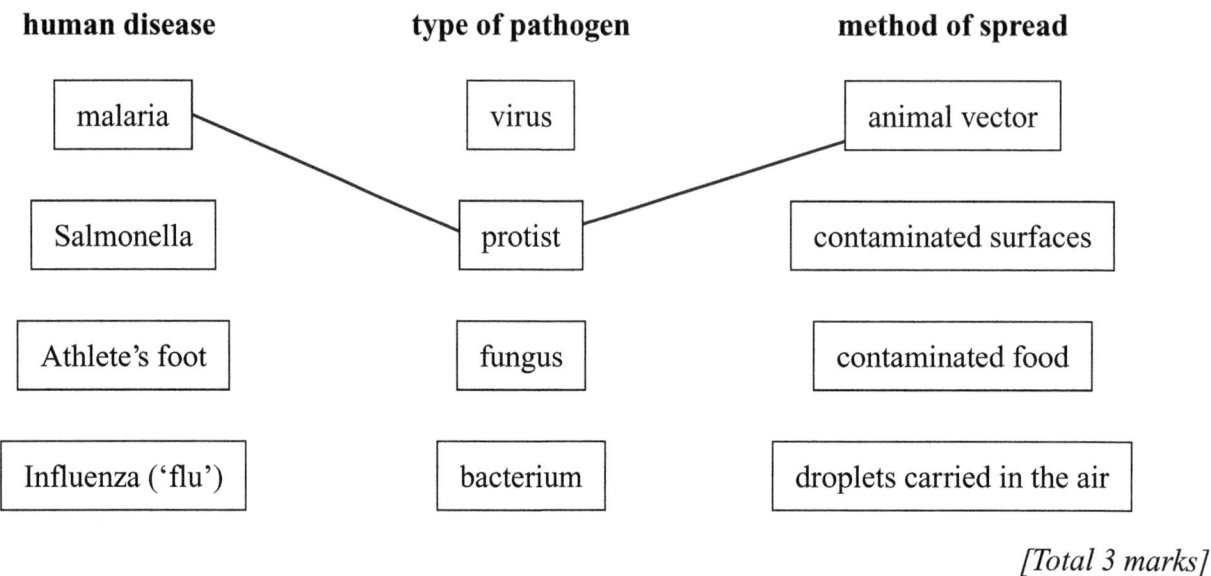

[Total 3 marks]

2 Plants are affected by different types of pathogens.

a) Chalara ash dieback is a disease which affects ash trees.
What type of pathogen causes ash dieback disease?
Place a tick (✓) in the box next to the correct answer.

bacterium ☐   virus ☐   fungus ☐   protist ☐

[1]

b) How is this pathogen spread between ash trees?

....

[1]

c) Crown gall disease also affects plants.
It is caused by a pathogen called '*Agrobacterium tumefaciens*'.

   i) What type of pathogen is '*Agrobacterium tumefaciens*'?

   ....

   [1]

   ii) How is this pathogen spread between plants?

   ....

   [1]

[Total 4 marks]

3 HIV is a disease that affects humans. It can be spread through unprotected sex.

a) What term is used to describe a disease that can be spread through unprotected sex?

....
[1]

b) Which of the following is another way that HIV can be spread?
Place a tick (✓) in the box next to the correct answer.

By receiving an infected blood transfusion. ☐

By bathing in contaminated water. ☐

By breathing in droplets produced when an infected person sneezes. ☐

By eating contaminated food. ☐

[1]

c) HIV can progress to the point where the infected person can't cope with other infections and cancers. What is this stage known as?

....
[1]

[Total 3 marks]

4 A farmer grows tobacco plants. He has noticed that the leaves of some of his plants have developed a patchy pattern. His plants are shown in the diagram below.

The farmer suspects that some of the plants have been infected with a pathogen.

a) Suggest the name of the pathogen that the plants have been infected with.

....
[1]

b) Suggest why not all of the farmer's tobacco plants have been infected with the pathogen.

....

....

....
[2]

[Total 3 marks]

Chapter B2 — Keeping Healthy

Defending Against Pathogens

1 Chemical and microbial defences help to prevent pathogens from entering the blood.

a) i) Explain how tears can act as a chemical defence against pathogens.

....

....
[2]

ii) Give **one** other chemical defence against pathogens in the human body.

....
[1]

b) Explain how bacteria naturally present in the gut help to defend the human body against pathogens.

....

....
[2]
[Total 5 marks]

2* A nurse in a hospital may come across many different pathogens in a single day. However, the pathogens do not always make the nurse ill. This is partly due to physical defences in the nurse's body, such as skin, mucus, cilia and platelets.

Describe and explain how the physical defences in the nurse's body help to prevent pathogens from causing infection.

....

....

....

....

....

....

....

....

....

....

....
[Total 6 marks]

Chapter B2 — Keeping Healthy

The Human Immune System

Warm-Up

Use the words on the right to complete the following sentences.

A .... can produce antibodies.

A .... has non-self antigens.

white blood cell

pathogen

1 The human immune response involves antibodies.

Which **one** of the following statements about antibodies is **true**?
Place a tick (✓) in the box next to the correct answer.

An antibody will bind to any type of antigen. ☐

An antibody will digest an antigen. ☐

An antibody will only bind to one type of antigen. ☐

An antibody will be destroyed by an antigen. ☐

[Total 1 mark]

2 The human immune system fights pathogens using a number of different methods.

a) The diagram on the right shows a pathogen being ingested by a white blood cell.
Describe what will happen to the pathogen next.

....
[1]

b) Other than the method shown above, describe **two** ways that white blood cells fight pathogens.

1. ....

2. ....
[2]

[Total 3 marks]

3 David was infected by a virus. The following year he was infected by the same virus again.
Explain why David was able to fight off the virus more quickly during the second infection.

....

....

....

....

[Total 3 marks]

Chapter B2 — Keeping Healthy

Reducing and Preventing the Spread of Disease

1 Gonorrhoea is a sexually transmitted infection. *(Grade 1-3)*

Suggest **one** way in which the spread of gonorrhoea could be reduced in people who are sexually active.

....

[Total 1 mark]

2 Many different methods are used to prevent the spread of a disease between crop plants. These include polyculture and chemical and biological control. *(Grade 3-4)*

a) Which of the following statements best describes polyculture?
Place a tick (✓) in the box next to the correct answer.

Growing plants in a greenhouse rather than outdoors. ☐

Growing different plants on the same patch of land at different times of the year. ☐

Growing a mixture of plants on the same patch of land at the same time. ☐

Using new varieties of plants which contain toxins that kill pests. ☐

[1]

b) Give **one** example of a chemical control method that could be used to control plant disease.

....

[1]

c) What is meant by the term 'biological control'?

....

....

[1]

[Total 3 marks]

3 A patient visits a nurse after cutting her finger. The nurse puts a dressing on the wound. *(Grade 4-5)*

a) Explain why the nurse washes her hands before she touches the patient.

....

....

[2]

b) Explain why the nurse sterilises the skin around the wound before she puts the dressing on.

....

....

[2]

[Total 4 marks]

Chapter B2 — Keeping Healthy

4 A farmer discovers that crops in one of her fields have been infected with a pathogen.

a) The farmer is deciding whether or not to destroy all of the infected plants.
Suggest **one** advantage and **one** disadvantage to the farmer of destroying the infected plants.

Advantage: ....

Disadvantage: ....
[2]

b) The farmer plans to use a crop rotation method in the future. Explain how this may help to reduce the number of plants that are infected with a pathogen in the future.

....

....

....
[2]
[Total 4 marks]

5 In 2001, there was a large outbreak of foot-and-mouth disease in the UK. Foot-and-mouth disease is a communicable disease that affects farm animals such as cows and sheep.

a) As a result of the outbreak, millions of animals had to be destroyed.
Suggest how this could have affected food sources in the UK.

....

....
[2]

b) During the outbreak, the government banned cows and sheep from the UK from being moved to other countries. Suggest why the government set up this ban.

....
[1]

c) It is possible to vaccinate animals against foot-and-mouth disease.
Explain how a vaccine might have helped to control the outbreak of the disease in 2001.

....

....

....
[3]
[Total 6 marks]

Exam Practice Tip
There are loads of different ways of reducing or preventing the spread of a disease. Don't let that scare you though. Just remember that all the methods have the same basic aim — to stop pathogens from getting from one organism to another. And don't forget that with any method there are always pros and cons to think about.

Chapter B2 — Keeping Healthy

Vaccinations

Warm-Up

Why are people given vaccinations? Underline the correct answer.

To help them get better if they are already ill.

To make it less likely that they will become ill in the future.

To get rid of their symptoms.

1 Children are often vaccinated against measles.

a) What is usually injected into the body during a vaccination?
Place a tick (✓) in the box next to the correct answer.

antibiotics ☐

antibodies ☐

dead or inactive pathogens ☐

active pathogens ☐

[1]

b) How should a child's body respond to a vaccination?

....
[1]
[Total 2 marks]

2 Two children become infected with the measles pathogen.
One child has been vaccinated against measles and the other has not.

The graph below shows how the concentration of the measles antibody in each child's bloodstream changes after infection with the measles pathogen.

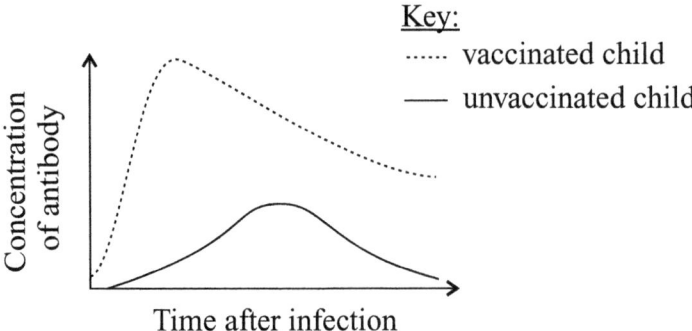

Using the graph, describe how antibody production differs between the vaccinated child and the unvaccinated child.

....

....

....
[Total 2 marks]

Chapter B2 — Keeping Healthy

Culturing Microorganisms — PRACTICAL

1 A scientist carried out an investigation into the effects of two different antibiotics on a culture of bacteria.

He poured agar jelly into a Petri dish. Once the agar was set, he coated it with bacteria. He then placed three different discs on the surface of the agar. Disc **A** was soaked in antibiotic **A**. Disc **B** was soaked in antibiotic **B**. Disc **C** was used as a control. A lid was taped onto the Petri dish and then it was left for two days to allow the bacteria to grow.

The diagram below shows the results of the experiment.

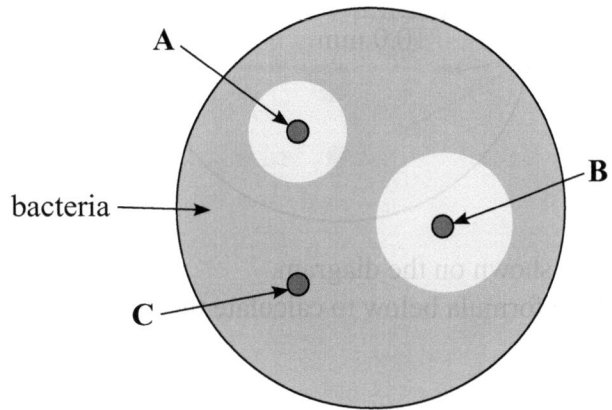

a) What should disc **C** have been soaked in before it was placed on the agar?
   Place a tick (✓) in the box next to the correct answer.

   Both antibiotic **A** and **B** ☐   Some of the bacterial culture ☐
   A third antibiotic ☐   Sterile water ☐

   [1]

b) What do the results of the experiment show?
   Place a tick (✓) in the box next to the correct answer.

   Antibiotic **A** was more effective than antibiotic **B** against the bacteria. ☐
   There was no difference between the effectiveness of the antibiotics against the bacteria. ☐
   Antibiotic **B** was more effective than antibiotic **A** against the bacteria. ☐
   Neither antibiotic **A** or antibiotic **B** were effective against the bacteria. ☐

   [1]

c) During the experiment, the scientist worked carefully to avoid contaminating the bacterial culture.

   i) Give **one** reason why it is important to avoid contaminating the bacterial culture.

   ....
   [1]

   ii) Give **two** things that the scientist should have done to avoid contaminating the bacterial culture.

   1. ....
   2. ....
   [2]

   [Total 5 marks]

Chapter B2 — Keeping Healthy

2 An investigation is carried out to examine the effect of a new antibiotic on a species of bacteria. A solution of agar is prepared and poured into a Petri dish. It is then left uncovered to dry.

a) Once the agar is dry, the plate is examined. The agar has been contaminated with several small bacterial colonies. These are shown on the diagram below.

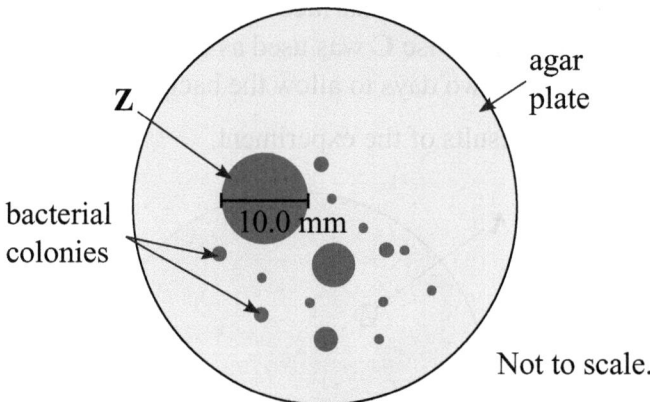

The diameter of colony **Z** is shown on the diagram.
Use this information and the formula below to calculate the area of colony **Z**.
area = πr^2
$\pi = 3.14$
Give your answer to 3 significant figures.

Area of colony Z = ... mm²
[2]

b) A fresh agar plate is prepared for the experiment.
Bacteria are spread over the surface of the agar.
Four discs soaked in the antibiotic to be tested are put on the surface of the agar.
After two days, the scientist measures the diameter of the clear zone around each disc.
Her results are shown in the table below.

Disc	1	2	3	4
Diameter of clear zone (mm)	18.0	6.80	17.9	18.7

The result for disc **2** is anomalous. Suggest **one** possible explanation for this anomalous result.

....

....
[1]
[Total 3 marks]

Exam Practice Tip
Make sure to write out all of your working when you're doing a calculation — it'll be easier to check your work and you might also pick up some marks for your working even if your final answer is wrong. If you need to measure anything in an exam question (e.g. the diameter of a bacterial colony) make sure that you're really careful with your measurements.

Chapter B2 — Keeping Healthy

Non-Communicable Diseases

Warm-Up

For each of the following statements, circle whether the statement is **true** or **false**.

Smoking is a risk factor for many diseases. — true / false

Exercising can reduce the risk of some non-communicable diseases. — true / false

Eating too little will not cause any health problems. — true / false

Many non-communicable diseases are caused by risk factors interacting. — true / false

---

1 Obesity is a non-communicable disease. *(Grade 1-3)*

Use words from the box to complete the following sentences about obesity.

| HIV | food | type 2 diabetes | exercise | malaria |

Obesity is linked to having too much ....

Being obese increases a person's risk of developing other non-communicable diseases,

such as ....

[Total 2 marks]

---

2 Non-communicable diseases are associated with risk factors. *(Grade 3-4)*

a) What is meant by a 'risk factor' for a disease?

....

....

[1]

b) Give **two** risk factors for non-communicable diseases that are related to a person's lifestyle.

1. ....

2. ....

[2]

c) Give **one** risk factor for non-communicable diseases that is **not** related to a person's lifestyle.

....

[1]

[Total 4 marks]

Chapter B2 — Keeping Healthy

3 People from poorer areas of the UK are more likely to smoke than people from richer areas.

a) Based on the information above, which of the following diseases is likely to be more common in poorer areas of the UK?

type 2 diabetes ☐   obesity ☐   lung cancer ☐   malaria ☐

[1]

b) Based on the information above, suggest how deaths related to smoking may vary in different areas of the world.

....

....

[1]

[Total 2 marks]

4 Jennifer visits a nurse for a health check.

The information that the nurse records about Jennifer is shown in the table below.

Weight description	Moderately obese
Blood pressure	Normal
Exercise habits	Regularly goes for long walks
Smoking habits	Smokes 15 cigarettes a day
Alcohol intake	Doesn't drink very often
Family history	Mother died from cardiovascular disease

a) Give **two** pieces of evidence from the table that suggest Jennifer may be at risk of developing cardiovascular disease.

1. ....

2. ....

[2]

b) Give **one** thing about Jennifer's lifestyle that may reduce her risk of developing cardiovascular disease.

....

[1]

c) Jennifer asks the nurse for some advice on how to reduce her risk of developing cardiovascular disease.
Suggest **one** piece of advice the nurse might give Jennifer about her **diet**.

....

[1]

[Total 4 marks]

Chapter B2 — Keeping Healthy

Interpreting Data on Disease

1 The graph below shows the incidence rate of lung cancer in males in Great Britain between 1990 and 2000. Incidence rate is a measure of how many new cases of the disease were diagnosed each year.

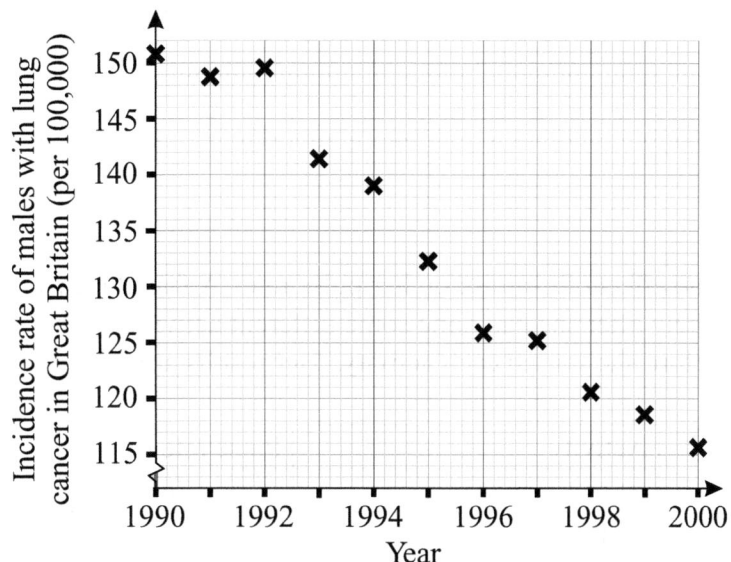

a) Describe the trend shown in the graph.

....

....
[1]

b) In what year was the incidence rate for lung cancer in males in Great Britain 139 per 100 000?

....
[1]

c) Between 1990 and 2000, there was a positive correlation between the number of males in Great Britain who smoked cigarettes and the incidence rate of lung cancer in males in Great Britain.

What does this mean? Place a tick (✓) in the box next to the correct answer.

Between 1990 and 2000, the number of males in Great Britain who smoked cigarettes...

... decreased. ☐ ... did not change. ☐

... increased. ☐ ... was the same as the incidence rate for lung cancer. ☐
[1]

d) In 2016, a student wrote an article based on the data in the graph.
The article concluded by stating that, 'fewer people are now getting lung cancer each year'.

Give **one** reason why it is not possible to draw this conclusion from the data in the graph.

....

....
[1]

[Total 4 marks]

Investigating Pulse Rate

1 A man's resting heart rate is 62 bpm. While swimming, his heart rate increases to 120 bpm. Describe how you could measure the man's recovery rate.

....

....

....

[Total 2 marks]

2 Lucy investigated the effect of exercise on her pulse rate. A friend measured her pulse rate at rest and immediately after she had done some different activities. She let her pulse return to its resting rate before she started each activity. Her results are shown in the table below.

Activity	Pulse rate (bpm)
At rest	76
Walking briskly 100 m	88
Jogging 200 m	128
Sprinting 200 m	156

a) Plot Lucy's results as a bar chart on the grid below.

At rest   Walking 100 m   Jogging 200 m   Sprinting 200 m

[2]

b) Lucy wants to repeat the experiment for a classmate to see if the results are similar to her own. Give **one** variable that she should keep constant when repeating this experiment.

....

....

[1]

[Total 3 marks]

Chapter B2 — Keeping Healthy

Treating Disease

1 A student has a sore throat. Her doctor says it is caused by a virus. *Grade 3-4*

a) The student says: "My sore throat can be treated with antibiotics."
Is the student correct? Give a reason for your answer.

....

....
[1]

b) The doctor could prescribe a drug to help the student with her sore throat.
Give **one** factor that the doctor would consider when deciding whether or not to prescribe a drug.

....
[1]
[Total 2 marks]

2 A hospital records the number of cases of infections that are caused by antibiotic-resistant bacteria each year. The figures for three years are shown in the table below. *Grade 4-5*

Year	2013	2014	2015
No. of infections	84	102	153

a) Describe the trend shown in the table.

....
[1]

b) Suggest why doctors in the hospital might be concerned about the trend shown in the table.

....

....
[2]

c) Suggest how the trend shown in the table might change the way that doctors prescribe drugs in the future.

....

....
[1]
[Total 4 marks]

Exam Practice Tip
Antibiotic resistance is a big deal in today's medicine world. It also crops up again in GCSE Combined Science — so make sure you know why it is becoming more common, why this is a problem, and what can be done to try and tackle it.

Chapter B2 — Keeping Healthy

Treating Cardiovascular Disease

Warm-Up

Fill in the gaps to complete the sentences. Choose **two** of the words or phrases below.

| lungs | blood vessels | heart | legs |

Cardiovascular diseases are diseases of the ....

and of the ....

1 Doctors were assessing the heart of a patient. They noticed that one of the main arteries supplying the heart muscle was narrowed.

Place a tick (✓) next to **two** pieces of lifestyle advice that the doctors may have given to the patient.

Eat a diet that is high in fat.	
Stop smoking.	
Exercise regularly.	
Drink more alcohol.	

[Total 1 mark]

2 A patient has been told he has cardiovascular disease. The doctors tell the patient he needs a surgical procedure to treat his condition. He is given information about having a stent inserted and about coronary bypass surgery. Some of the information is shown in the table below.

	Stent	Coronary bypass surgery
Time surgery takes	30 minutes - 2 hours	3-6 hours
Length of hospital stay	0-1 days	7 days or more
Approximate recovery time	1 week	6-12 weeks
Other information	Repeat surgery may be needed if artery narrows again	Less likely to need repeat surgery

After discussing the options with his doctor, the patient chooses to have a stent inserted rather than have coronary bypass surgery.

Using information from the table, evaluate why the patient may have made this choice.

....

....

....

....

[Total 4 marks]

Chapter B2 — Keeping Healthy

Developing New Medicines

1 New drugs have to undergo preclinical and clinical testing before they can be used.

a) i) What are new drugs tested on during preclinical trials?
Place a tick (✓) in the box next to the correct answer.

- healthy human volunteers ☐
- cultured human cells and dead animals ☐
- patients in a hospital ☐
- cultured human cells and live animals ☐

[1]

ii) Give **one** factor which is investigated during the preclinical testing of drugs.

....

[1]

If a drug passes all of the preclinical trials then it is tested in clinical trials.

b) Before the new drug can be given to people suffering from the illness that it is designed to treat, it must be tested for harmful side effects. Who is this testing carried out on?

....

[1]

c) Clinical trials of new drugs often involve the use of a placebo.

i) What is a placebo?

....

....

[1]

ii) Explain why some patients in a clinical trial are given the drug and others are given a placebo.

....

....

[2]

iii) Clinical trials of new drugs can be blind, double blind or open-label.
Who knows which participants are receiving the drug in a **blind trial**?
Place a tick (✓) in the box next to the correct answer.

- patients and doctor ☐
- doctor only ☐
- patients only ☐
- neither the patients nor the doctor ☐

[1]

[Total 7 marks]

Enzymes

1 The diagram on the right shows an enzyme. *(Grade 1-3)*

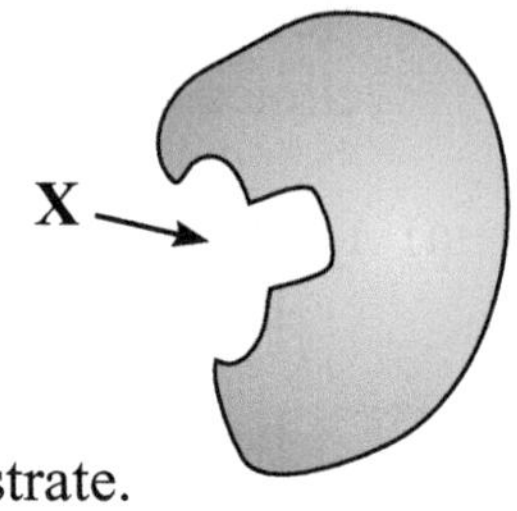

a) Name the part of the enzyme labelled **X** on the diagram.

....
[1]

b) The enzyme in the diagram above catalyses a reaction that breaks apart a substrate. Which of the following diagrams shows the reaction catalysed by this enzyme? Place a tick (✓) in the box next to the correct answer.

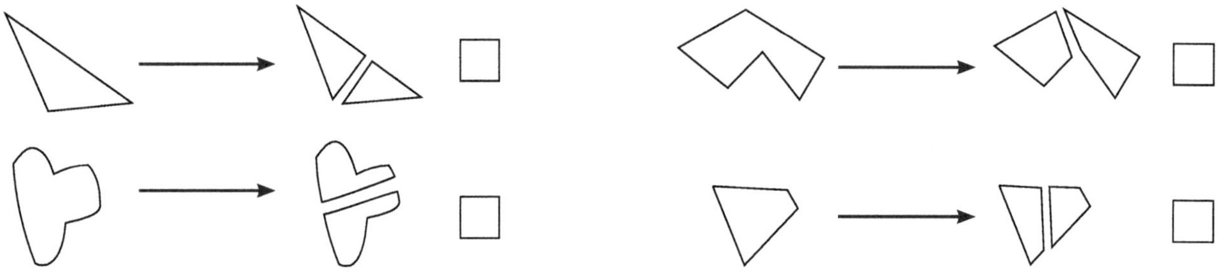

[1]

[Total 2 marks]

2 A reaction is catalysed by an enzyme. The graph on the right shows how temperature affects the rate of this reaction. *(Grade 4-5)*

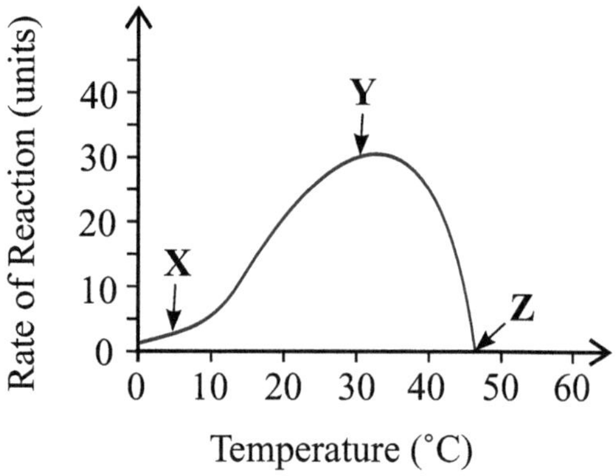

a) Look at points **X** and **Y** on the graph.

Describe the relationship between rate of reaction and temperature between points **X** and **Y**.

....
[1]

b) Using the graph above, estimate the optimum temperature for this reaction.

....
[1]

c) Explain why the reaction has stopped at point **Z**.

....
....
....
[3]

[Total 5 marks]

3 The enzyme amylase breaks down starch to sugar.

A student investigated the effect of pH on amylase activity. He followed this method:
1. Put a drop of iodine solution in each well of a spotting tile.
2. Add amylase and buffer solution to a test tube.
3. Add starch solution to the test tube.
4. Take a sample of the test tube mixture every 30 seconds. Add the sample to a well on the spotting tile.

Iodine solution is a browny-orange colour. It turns blue-black in the presence of starch. The student recorded the colour of the iodine solution after each sample was added to the spotting tile. The results for pH 4 are shown in the table below.

Time (s)	Colour
30	Blue-black
60	Blue-black
90	Blue-black
120	Browny-orange
150	Browny-orange

a) At what time point did the student first record that there was no starch left in the mixture?

....

[1]

The student repeated the experiment at different pH values.

b) At pH 6, the reaction took 150 s to complete.
Calculate the rate of reaction at pH 6.

Use the equation: $\text{rate} = \dfrac{1}{\text{time taken}}$

Give your answer to 2 significant figures.

rate = ... s^{-1}

[1]

c) Give **two** variables that the student should control in this experiment.

1. ....

2. ....

[2]

d) The student wants to improve the accuracy of his results.
Describe **one** way that the experiment could be improved to give more accurate results.

....

....

[1]

[Total 5 marks]

Exam Practice Tip

Make sure you learn how pH, temperature and substrate concentration affect enzyme activity — examiners just love asking questions about it. pH and temperature have similar effects. They increase the rate of the reaction up to an optimum — above the optimum, the reaction rate decreases. It's a bit different with substrate concentration though.

  Chapter B3 — Living Together — Food and Ecosystems

Photosynthesis

1 Use words from the box to complete the following passage about photosynthesis.

| enzymes | decrease | increase | substrates | products |

Increasing the carbon dioxide concentration in a greenhouse will usually

.... the rate of photosynthesis.

This is because photosynthesis is controlled by .... and carbon dioxide

is one of its ....

[Total 3 marks]

2 Photosynthesis involves several chemical reactions, but takes place in two main stages.

a) Complete the table below to show the main inputs and outputs of each stage of photosynthesis.

	Inputs	Output(s)
First stage of photosynthesis	1. .... 2. Chlorophyll 3.	1. .... 2. Hydrogen ions
Second stage of photosynthesis	1. .... 2. Hydrogen ions	1. Glucose

[4]

b) Give **two** ways in which plants use the glucose they produce during photosynthesis.

1. ....

2. ....

[2]

c) Place a tick (✓) in the box that explains why photosynthesis is an endothermic process.

Energy is taken in during photosynthesis. ☐

Energy is released during photosynthesis. ☐

Energy is made during photosynthesis. ☐

Energy is broken down during photosynthesis. ☐

[1]

[Total 7 marks]

Investigating Photosynthesis — PRACTICAL

1 A student wants to test a leaf for the presence of starch. *(Grade 3-4)*

a) Which of the following does the student need to use to find out if the leaf contains starch?
Place a tick (✓) in the box next to the correct answer.

pH indicator ☐   biuret reagent ☐   Benedict's reagent ☐   iodine solution ☐

[1]

b) Before a leaf is tested for starch, the chlorophyll must be removed.
Describe a method that the student could use to remove chlorophyll from the leaf.

....

....
[2]

c) The student tests the leaf and finds that it contains starch.
Describe the result you would expect the student to see.

....
[1]

[Total 4 marks]

2* A student wants to show that carbon dioxide is a requirement of photosynthesis.
Describe a method that she could use to do this. Include details of any variables
she should control and explain the results you would expect her to see. *(Grade 4-5)*

....

....

....

....

....

....

....

....

....

....

[Total 6 marks]

Exam Practice Tip

Don't panic when you get to a 6 mark question in the exams. Read the question through carefully, then stop and think before you answer. First work out what the question is asking you to write about. Then write down the points you want to make, in an order that makes sense. Make sure you make enough points to get yourself as many marks as possible.

    Chapter B3 — Living Together — Food and Ecosystems

Investigating the Rate of Photosynthesis

PRACTICAL

1 A student did an experiment to see how the rate of photosynthesis depends on light intensity. She measured the volume of oxygen produced by pondweed at different intensities of light. The table below shows her results. A diagram of her apparatus is shown on the right.

Relative light intensity	1	2	3	4	5	6	7	8	9	10
Volume of oxygen produced in 10 minutes (cm^3)	8	12	18	25	31	13	42	48	56	61

a) State the dependent variable and the independent variable in this experiment.

Dependent variable: ....

Independent variable: ....

[2]

b) State **two** factors that should be kept constant during this experiment.

1. ....

2. ....

[2]

c) Plot the student's results on the grid on the right.

[3]

d) One of the student's results is anomalous.
At which relative light intensity is the result anomalous?

Relative light intensity = ...

[1]

e) Describe what the student's results show about the relationship between light intensity and rate of photosynthesis.

....

[1]

[Total 9 marks]

Chapter B3 — Living Together — Food and Ecosystems

Diffusion, Osmosis and Active Transport

Warm-Up

The diagram on the right shows two cells. Draw an arrow between the cells to show the direction in which carbon dioxide will diffuse.

carbon dioxide concentration = 0.2% | carbon dioxide concentration = 1.5% ← cell

1 Osmosis is a form of diffusion. *Grade 3-4*

a) Use words from the box to complete the following definition of osmosis.

| sugar | lower | higher | water | oxygen |

Osmosis is the movement of .... molecules across a partially permeable membrane from a region of .... water concentration to a region of .... water concentration.

[3]

b) In which **one** of these scenarios is osmosis occurring? Place a tick (✓) in the box next to the correct answer.

A plant is absorbing water from the soil. ☐

Sugar is being taken up into the blood from the gut. ☐

Water is moving from the mouth down to the stomach. ☐

Oxygen is entering the blood from the lungs. ☐

[1]
[Total 4 marks]

2 Glucose molecules can be absorbed from the gut into the blood by active transport. *Grade 4-5*

a) Which of these statements about active transport is correct? Place a tick (✓) in the box next to the correct answer.

It's a type of diffusion. ☐

It can only occur down a concentration gradient. ☐

It needs energy from respiration. ☐

It needs energy from photosynthesis. ☐

[1]

b) Suggest why active transport is used to take up glucose from the gut into the blood.

....

....

[2]
[Total 3 marks]

Chapter B3 — Living Together — Food and Ecosystems

Transport in Plants and Prokaryotes

1 Leaves are adapted for gas exchange. The diagram below shows a cross-section of a leaf.

a) Name the openings in the leaf labelled **X**.

....
[1]

b) Describe the movement of gases into and out of the leaf that are a result of photosynthesis taking place.

....

....
[2]

c) Having entered the leaf, describe how gases move into plant cells.

....

....
[2]

d) Some prokaryotes also photosynthesise.
Suggest why these prokaryotes don't need specialised gas exchange structures, such as leaves.

....

....
[2]

[Total 7 marks]

2 The diagram below shows a plant root hair cell. It is surrounded by mineral ions (NO_3^- and K^+).

a) Plants get nitrogen from NO_3^- ions. What type of molecule do plants need nitrogen to produce?

....
[1]

b) Explain why the root hair cell needs to use active transport to absorb the mineral ions.

....

....
[2]

[Total 3 marks]

Chapter B3 — Living Together — Food and Ecosystems

Investigating Diffusion and Osmosis

Warm-Up

Use words on the right to complete the following passage about osmosis.

A potato chip was placed in a sucrose solution. The potato chip gained mass.
This is because water moved .... the potato chip by osmosis.
This means that the sucrose solution had a ....
concentration of water molecules than the potato chip.

out of
into
higher
lower

1 A student made up some agar jelly using phenolphthalein indicator and dilute sodium hydroxide (an alkali). He cut the agar jelly into cubes of different sizes. He put the different sizes of cubes into separate beakers. Then he poured a small amount of dilute acid into each beaker.

Grade 4-5

Phenolphthalein is pink in solutions above pH 8 and colourless in solutions below pH 8.

a) Explain why the agar cubes gradually changed from pink to colourless after the acid was added to each beaker.

....

....
[2]

The student timed how long it took for the agar cubes in each beaker to turn colourless. His results are shown below.

Beaker	Cube surface area (mm^2)	Time taken for colour loss (s)
1	600	540
2	486	350
3	216	140
4	96	64

b) Describe the relationship between the surface area of the cube and the time taken for the colour loss in each cube.

....

....
[1]

c) Describe what the student could do to increase his confidence in his results.

....

....
[1]

[Total 4 marks]

2 A student did an experiment to see the effect of different sucrose solutions on pieces of potato.

- He cut five equal-sized chips from a raw potato and measured the mass of each chip.
- Each chip was placed in a beaker containing a different concentration of sucrose solution.
- The mass of each chip was measured again after 1 hour. The results are shown below.

	Beaker				
	1	2	3	4	5
Concentration of sucrose solution (M)	0.1	0.3	0.5	0.7	0.9
% change in mass of potato chip	+9	+2	−3	+19	....

a) The mass of the potato chip in Beaker 5 was 10.0 g before the experiment and 9.3 g afterwards. Calculate the percentage change in mass of the potato chip in Beaker 5.

.... %
[2]

b) One of the results shown in the table above is anomalous.
State the number of the beaker with the anomalous result. Explain your answer.

....

....
[2]

c) Describe what the student should do about the anomalous result.

....

....
[1]

d) Ignoring the anomalous result, water moved into the potato cylinders in **two** of the beakers.
State the numbers of these **two** beakers. Give a reason for your answer.

Beakers: ....

Reason: ....
[1]

[Total 6 marks]

Exam Practice Tip

Examiners just love asking questions about potato chips and osmosis — so make sure you understand what's going on in the experiment above. If you get a question on a similar experiment in the exam, the method might not be exactly the same (e.g. it might use apple chips rather than potato chips, or look at the change in chip length rather than mass). Don't panic though — it'll just be a case of applying what you've learnt to a slightly different context.

Chapter B3 — Living Together — Food and Ecosystems

Xylem and Phloem

Warm-Up

The diagrams show a phloem tube and a xylem tube.
In the spaces below, write down which one is the phloem tube and which one is the xylem tube.

A: ....

B: ....

1   Xylem and phloem transport substances through a plant.

a) What does the xylem transport?
   Place a tick (✓) in the box next to **two** correct answers.

   mineral ions ☐   protein ☐   sugar ☐   water ☐   starch ☐

   [2]

b) Which statement about transport in the phloem is correct?
   Place a tick (✓) in the box next to the correct answer.

   It only occurs in the leaves. ☐

   It is called transpiration. ☐

   It moves sugar around the plant. ☐

   It only moves substances upwards from the roots. ☐

   [1]
   [Total 3 marks]

2   Use words from the box to complete the following passage about transport in plants. Each word may be used once or not at all.

| transpiration | translocation | active transport | condensation | evaporation |

The process by which water is lost from a plant is called ....

It is caused by the .... and diffusion of water from a plant's surface.

The transport of sugars around the plant is called ....

[Total 3 marks]

Chapter B3 — Living Together — Food and Ecosystems

Stomata

1 The diagram below shows part of the surface of a leaf. *Grade 4-5*

a) Name the structures labelled **X** and **Y** in the diagram.

X: .... Y: ....
[2]

b) Explain how the structures labelled **Y** can affect how much water is lost from the plant.

....

....

....

....
[4]

[Total 6 marks]

PRACTICAL

2 A student is preparing a microscope slide to view xylem cells.
She begins by placing a plant stem upright in a beaker containing a solution of eosin dye. After a few hours, she takes a thin cross-section of the stem. *Grade 4-5*

a) Explain why she places the plant stem upright in the dye before taking a cross-section of the stem.

....

....

....
[3]

b) The student also wants to examine the stomata on the underside of a leaf.
Describe how she could prepare a slide to view the structure of the stomata under a microscope.

....

....

....
[3]

[Total 6 marks]

Exam Practice Tip

The best way to learn how to prepare microscope slides of different types of cells is to do it yourself. Make sure you get plenty of practice in class, so that when it comes to the exam, you'll be totally prepared for whatever comes up.

Chapter B3 — Living Together — Food and Ecosystems

Transpiration Rate

Warm-Up

Which of the following would **decrease** the rate of transpiration of a plant growing outdoors? Circle the correct answer.

a very windy day   bright sunshine   frosty conditions

1 Environmental conditions can affect a plant's transpiration rate. *(Grade 3-4)*

a) Give **one** reason why a plant growing outside might transpire faster in the summer than in the winter.

....
[1]

b) Explain why transpiration is usually slower at night than it is during the day.

....

....
[2]
[Total 3 marks]

2 A student is investigating the effect of temperature on the rate of transpiration in a pot plant. *(Grade 4-5)*

- The student measures the mass of a plant in its pot.
- She leaves the plant at a temperature of 22 °C for 24 hours.
- She then measures the plant's mass again.

Her results are shown in the table on the right.

Mass of plant and pot (g)	
Before	After
951	945

a) Use the student's results to estimate the plant's transpiration rate.

.... g/day
[1]

b) Give **one** reason why your answer to part **a)** is only an estimate of the plant's transpiration rate.

....
[1]

c) The student repeats the experiment, but leaves the plant at a temperature of 15 °C for 24 hours. Suggest and explain what her results will show.

....

....

....
[2]
[Total 4 marks]

Chapter B3 — Living Together — Food and Ecosystems

Using a Potometer

1. A group of students were investigating the effect of air flow on the rate of transpiration. To do so, they measured the water uptake of a plant in still and moving air using the apparatus shown below. The rate of water uptake is assumed to be equal to the transpiration rate.

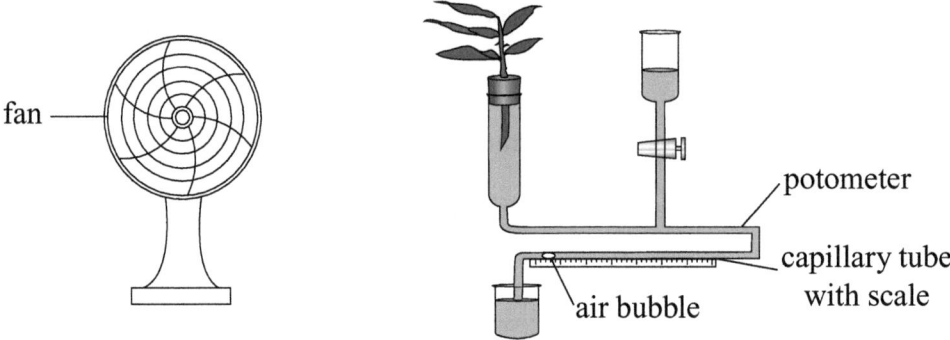

a) Describe how the rate of water uptake can be measured using the potometer shown above.

....
....
....
....
[3]

The table below shows the students' results.

	Repeat	1	2	3	4	Mean
Water uptake in 1 hour (mm³)	Still Air	2400	2400	2000	1600	2100
	Moving Air	4000	3600	4600	3800	4000

b) Describe the relationship between air flow around the plant and transpiration rate.

....
[1]

c) Explain the effect of air flow on the rate of transpiration.

....
....
....
[2]

d) Calculate the **range** for the results in **moving air**.

range = ... mm³
[1]

[Total 7 marks]

Chapter B3 — Living Together — Food and Ecosystems

Ecosystems and Interactions Between Organisms

Warm-Up

Biotic factors are the living factors in an environment. Circle **three** biotic factors below.

moisture level   competition   temperature   wind direction   pathogens   predators

---

1 Ecosystems are organised into different levels.

a) Put a tick (✓) in the box next to the correct definition of a community.

A single organism. ☐

All the organisms of different species living in a habitat. ☐

All the organisms of one species in a habitat. ☐

All the organisms living in a habitat along with all the non-living conditions. ☐

[1]

b) Put a tick (✓) in the box next to the correct definition of a population.

A single organism. ☐

All the organisms of different species living in a habitat. ☐

All the organisms of one species in a habitat. ☐

All the organisms living in a habitat along with all the non-living conditions. ☐

[1]

[Total 2 marks]

---

2 A new pathogen is introduced into a population of flowering plants.

a) Describe how the introduction of the new pathogen is likely to affect the plant population.

....

....

[1]

b) Bees in the ecosystem rely on the flowering plants for a source of food.
Explain how the introduction of the pathogen is likely to affect the bee population.

....

....

[2]

[Total 3 marks]

Chapter B3 — Living Together — Food and Ecosystems

Abiotic Factors and Investigating Distribution

PRACTICAL

1   A group of students used 1 m² quadrats to compare the population sizes of buttercups in two areas of a field. They collected data from three randomly placed quadrats in each area. Their results are shown in the table below.

	Quadrat 1	Quadrat 2	Quadrat 3	Mean	Range
Area 1	15	14	13	14	2
Area 2	26	23	18	X	Y

a) Why is it important that the quadrats were placed randomly in the field?
    Put a tick (✓) in the box next to the correct answer.

   To avoid disturbing too much of the field. ☐

   To make the sampling process quicker. ☐

   To make sure the sample represented the general features of the whole field. ☐

   To make sure that every single part of the field was sampled. ☐

   [1]

b) Calculate the values of **X** and **Y**.
    Give the value of **X** to 2 significant figures.

    X = ...

    Y = ...
    [3]

c) The students notice that the buttercups in **Area 1** were growing in the shade.
    The buttercups in **Area 2** were growing in full sun.
    A student says:
    "The lower light intensity has affected the growth of the buttercups in **Area 1**."
    Do you agree with the student? Give a reason for your answer.

    ....

    ....

    ....
    [1]
    [Total 5 marks]

Exam Practice Tip

Make sure you take the right numbers from the data when you're carrying out calculations like the ones above — you don't want to lose marks just for writing down a number wrong. And remember, the first significant figure of a number is the first digit that's not zero. The second and third significant figures come straight after (even if they're zeros).

Chapter B3 — Living Together — Food and Ecosystems

Investigating Ecosystems — PRACTICAL

1 Two groups of students investigated the population size of limpets on a beach. The beach had an area of 1750 m².

a) The first group of students took random samples along the beach using 1 m² quadrats. They found a mean of 14 limpets per quadrat.
Estimate the total number of limpets on the beach based on the first group's findings.

.... limpets
[1]

b) The second group of students took random samples along the beach using quadrats with an area of 0.25 m². They found a mean of 5 limpets per quadrat.
Estimate the total number of limpets on the beach based on the second group's findings.

.... limpets
[2]

[Total 3 marks]

2 Students used a capture-recapture method to estimate the population size of a species of snail living in a pond. Their results are shown below.

Number in 1st sample	Number in 2nd sample	Number of marked snails in 2nd sample
12	15	3

a) Describe the steps the students should have taken to collect the data in the table.

....

....

....

....

....
[4]

b) Estimate the population size of the snail species from the data in table above.
Use the equation:

$$\text{population size} = \frac{\text{number in first sample} \times \text{number in second sample}}{\text{number in second sample marked}}$$

population size = ... snails
[1]

[Total 5 marks]

Chapter B3 — Living Together — Food and Ecosystems

PRACTICAL: More on Investigating Ecosystems

1 The diagram below shows a transect line. It is being used to record the distribution of four types of plant in a field. *Grade 1-3*

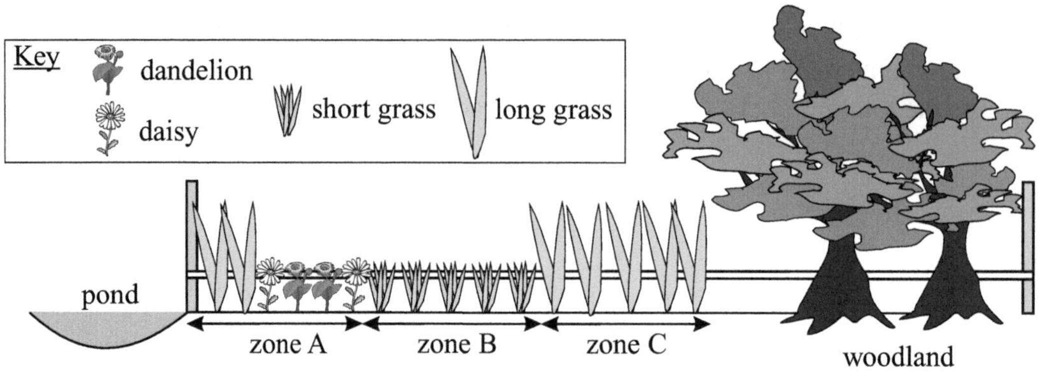

Give **two** pieces of equipment that may have been used to help collect the information shown in the diagram.

1. .... 2. ....

[Total 2 marks]

2 Samantha is using a key to identify some butterflies based on the markings on their wings. Part of the key is shown below. *Grade 3-4*

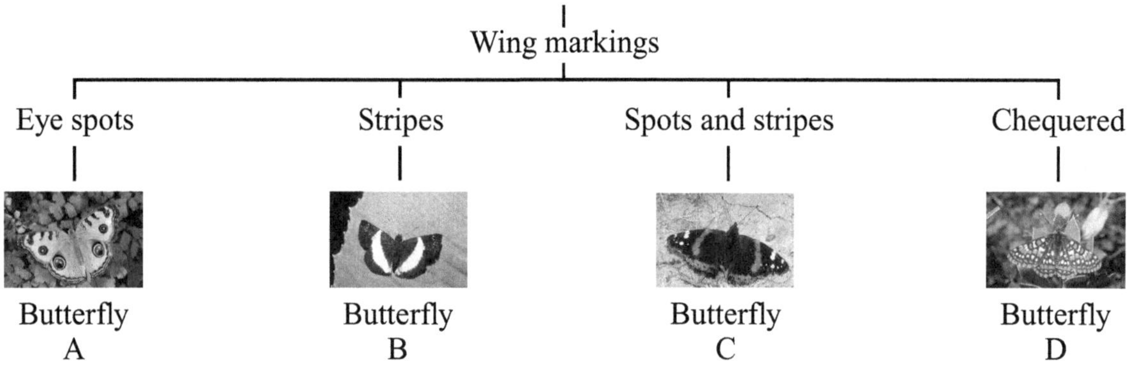

Samantha is given the photograph shown below.

Samantha uses the key to identify the butterfly species in the photograph — it is a Red Admiral. Based on the wing markings in the key, which of the butterflies in the key is a Red Admiral butterfly? Explain your answer.

....

....

[Total 2 marks]

Investigating Factors Affecting Distribution

PRACTICAL

1 Abiotic factors can affect the distribution of organisms.

a) Suggest **one** piece of equipment that could be used to measure each of the following abiotic factors.

Temperature: ....

Soil pH: ....

Light intensity: ....
[3]

b) Apart from the abiotic factors given in part **a)**, suggest **one** other abiotic factor which may affect the distribution of a species.

....
[1]

[Total 4 marks]

PRACTICAL

2 Blood worms usually live in highly polluted water. Stonefly larvae can only survive in clean water.

a) What term is used to describe organisms that can be used to assess the level of pollution in an ecosystem?

....
[1]

b) Describe how you could use blood worms and stonefly larvae to assess the level of pollution along a river. Include details on how you could sample the organisms.

....

....

....

....

....

....
[4]

[Total 5 marks]

Exam Practice Tip

The organisms that you can use to assess the pollution of an ecosystem depend on the type of ecosystem that you're studying. So don't be alarmed if you get some examples in the exam that you've never heard of. Just apply what you know to the question. Also, make sure that you're confident with sampling techniques for different types of organisms.

Chapter B3 — Living Together — Food and Ecosystems

Food Chains and Food Webs

Warm-Up

On the food chain below, circle the **producer**.

seaweed → fish → shark → whale

---

1 A woodland food chain is shown in the diagram below. *(Grade 1-3)*

green plants → greenflies → blue tits → sparrowhawk

a) Green plants make their own food. What process do they use to do this?

....
[1]

b) In the woodland food chain shown above, biomass is transferred from the green plants to the greenflies. How is this shown in the diagram?

....
[1]
[Total 2 marks]

---

2 A food web is shown on the right. *(Grade 4-5)*

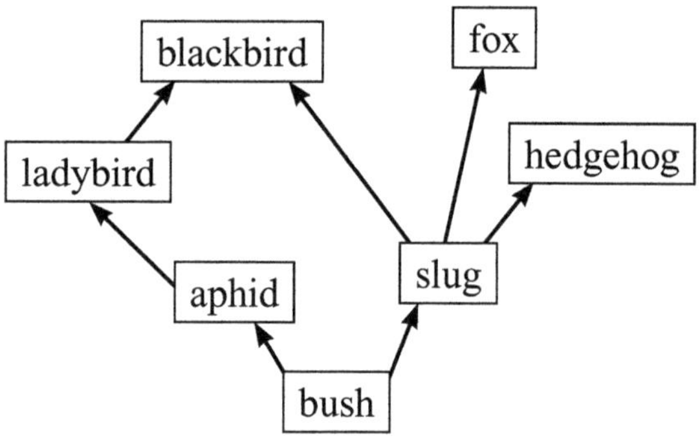

a) The organisms in the food web are interdependent. Explain what 'interdependent' means.

....

....

....
[1]

b) Explain what is likely to happen to the size of the ladybird population if the population of blackbirds decreases.

....

....
[2]

c) Explain what might happen to the size of the hedgehog population if the population of blackbirds decreases.

....

....
[2]
[Total 5 marks]

Making and Breaking Biological Molecules

1 Producers take in carbon from the air and nitrogen compounds from the soil.

Put a tick (✓) in the box that correctly states how consumers take in carbon and nitrogen compounds.

From the air and the soil. ☐

By eating producers only. ☐

By eating other consumers only. ☐

By eating both producers and other consumers. ☐

[Total 1 mark]

2 The diagrams below show how different molecules are broken down.

carbohydrate → **A**

protein → **B**

C → **D**, fatty acids

a) Name the molecules labelled **A-D** in the diagrams above.

A ....

B ....

C ....

D ....

[4]

b) Explain why the breakdown of large molecules into smaller molecules is necessary for consumers.

....

....

....

[2]

[Total 6 marks]

Chapter B3 — Living Together — Food and Ecosystems

Testing for Biological Molecules

Warm-Up

Put a tick (✓) in the box next to the correct test for **glucose**.

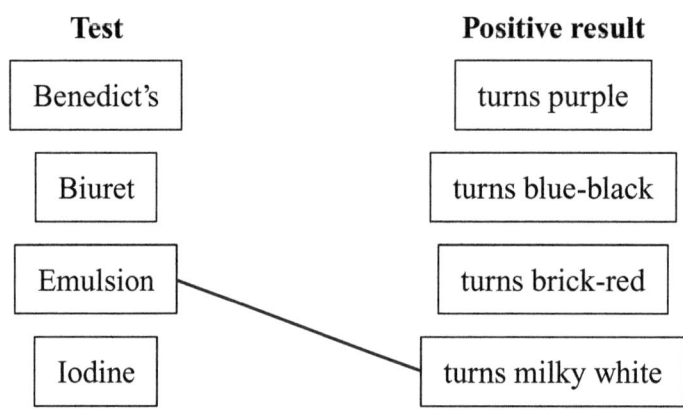

1   Many food tests involve a colour change.

Draw **one** line to match each of the following tests to its positive result.
One line has been drawn for you.

Test	Positive result
Benedict's	turns purple
Biuret	turns blue-black
Emulsion	turns brick-red
Iodine	turns milky white

(Emulsion is connected to turns milky white)

[Total 2 marks]

2   A student is analysing the nutrient content of egg whites.

a) Describe a test the student could do to find out if fat is present in a sample of the egg whites.

....

....

....

[4]

b) Describe how the student could test for protein in a sample of the egg whites.

....

....

....

[3]

[Total 7 marks]

Cycles in Ecosystems

1 A simplified version of the carbon cycle is shown below.

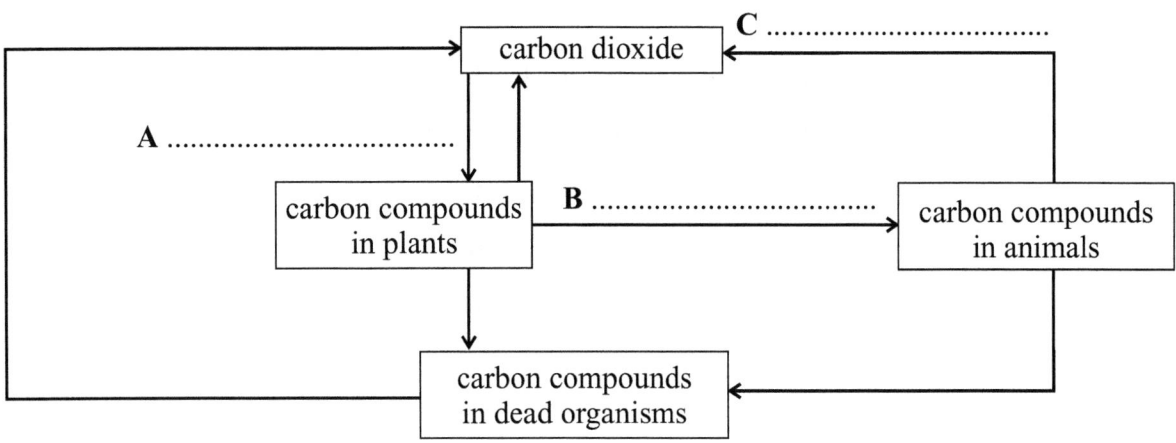

Complete the diagram above.
Fill in the labels **A**, **B** and **C** using words from the box.

| decay | respiration | eating | photosynthesis | precipitation |

[Total 3 marks]

2 The carbon cycle describes how carbon moves between organisms and their environment.

a) Explain how microorganisms in the soil release carbon from dead matter.

....

....

....

[3]

b) Describe how combustion moves carbon between organisms and the environment.

....

....

[2]

[Total 5 marks]

Exam Practice Tip

Make sure you know all of the carbon cycle, not just bits of it. Try sketching out the whole cycle to help you remember it. First write out the different parts, e.g. the air, plants, etc. Then think of the different processes that move carbon around between these parts, e.g. respiration. Draw arrows to show the direction in which these processes move carbon.

     Chapter B3 — Living Together — Food and Ecosystems

More on Cycles in Ecosystems

Warm-Up

Find the **three** types of precipitation in the wordsearch below and circle them.

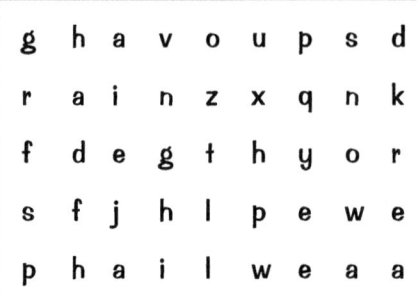

1   The diagram on the right shows how water is transferred in the water cycle.

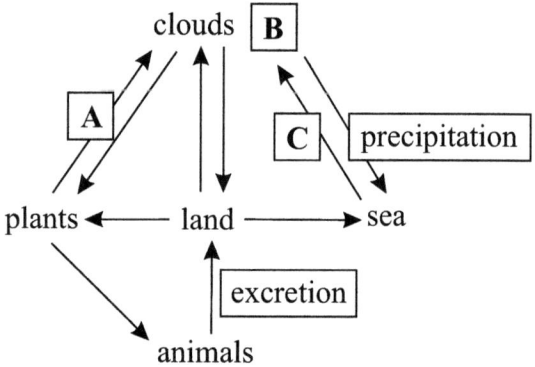

a) Name the processes represented by the letters **A**, **B** and **C** in the diagram.

A ....

B ....

C ....
[3]

b) What is meant by the term 'precipitation'?

....
[1]

c) Animals obtain some water from plants.
State how water is transferred from plants to animals.

....
[1]

d) Animals return water to the soil via excretion.

i) Explain what is meant by the term 'excretion'.

....
[1]

ii) The soil is unable to absorb all the water that falls on it.
Describe what happens to excess water that is not absorbed by the soil.

....

....
[1]
[Total 7 marks]

Chapter B3 — Living Together — Food and Ecosystems

Chapter B4 — Using Food and Controlling Growth

Respiration

Warm-Up

Use the words on the right to complete the sentences.

Respiration transfers energy from the breakdown of ....

Respiration makes a substance called ....

ATP

glucose

1 Respiration is an important chemical reaction. *Grade 3-4*

a) Use words from the box to complete the following sentences about respiration.

| exothermic | from | endothermic | all | to | some |

Respiration reactions are carried out by .... living cells.

Respiration is an .... reaction.

It transfers energy .... the environment.

[3]

The picture on the right shows a gull.

b) Give **two** examples of how a gull uses the energy transferred by respiration.

1. ....

2. ....

[2]

[Total 5 marks]

2 Students investigated the effect of two different substrates on the rate of aerobic respiration in yeast. Their results are shown in the table below. *Grade 4-5*

a) Calculate the rate of respiration for yeast with fructose.

.... cm^3/min

[1]

Substrate	Volume of CO_2 produced in 20 minutes (cm^3)	Rate of respiration (cm^3/min)
Glucose	9.8	0.49
Fructose	5.8	

b) Besides the substrate, which of the following is an input needed for aerobic respiration? Place a tick (✓) in the box next to the correct answer.

water ☐   carbon dioxide ☐   lactic acid ☐   oxygen ☐

[1]

[Total 2 marks]

More on Respiration

1 Cellular respiration can occur either aerobically or anaerobically. Both types of respiration produce ATP, but in different amounts.

a) i) Name a substance that is broken down in both aerobic and anaerobic respiration.

....
[1]

ii) Name a substance that is used in aerobic respiration but not in anaerobic respiration.

....
[1]

b) Give **one** reason why it may be more beneficial for the body to use aerobic respiration to transfer energy most of the time, rather than using anaerobic respiration.

....

....
[1]
[Total 3 marks]

2 Waterlogged soil contains little or no oxygen.

Cells in the roots of plants growing in waterlogged soil continue to respire.
Suggest what **two** substances are produced when these cells respire. Explain your answer.

....

....
[Total 3 marks]

3 The process used to make alcoholic beer involves yeast respiring anaerobically.

a) Complete the word equation for the respiration reaction that takes place when making beer.

.... → ethanol (alcohol) + ...
[2]

b) During the beer-making process, it is important that the mixture containing yeast is held in a sealed container. This is so that no oxygen can enter the container. Suggest why it's important that no oxygen enters the container during the beer-making process.

....

....
[2]
[Total 4 marks]

Chapter B4 — Using Food and Controlling Growth

The Cell Cycle and Mitosis

1 The diagram below shows a cell during the cell cycle.

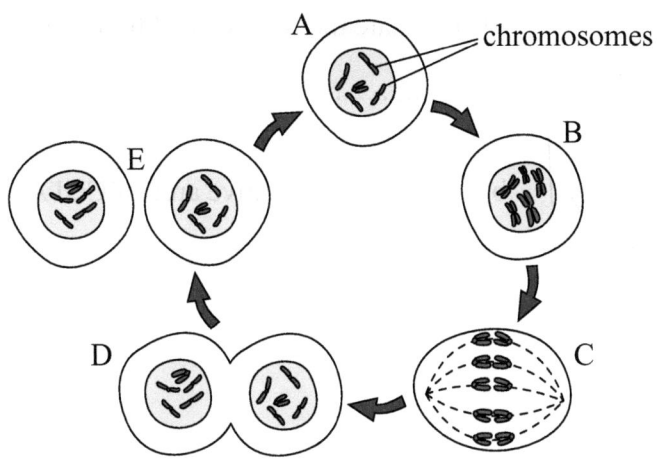

a) Cell **A** is preparing to divide.

i) What is happening to the chromosomes in cell **A**?
Place a tick (✓) in the box next to the correct answer.

The chromosomes are dividing. ☐

The chromosomes are being copied. ☐

The chromosomes are getting longer. ☐

The chromosomes are splitting. ☐

[1]

ii) What else is happening in cell **A**?
Place a tick (✓) in the box next to the correct answer.

The number of mitochondria is increasing. ☐

The number of ribosomes is decreasing. ☐

The nucleus is dividing. ☐

The cell is shrinking. ☐

[1]

iii) Name the stage of the cell cycle that cell **A** is in.

....

[1]

b) How do the two cells produced at stage **E** compare to cell **A**?
Place a tick (✓) in the box next to the correct answer.

They are genetically different. ☐

They are genetically similar. ☐

They are genetically identical. ☐

[1]

[Total 4 marks]

Microscopy

1 Scientific drawings of two cells during different stages of mitosis are shown below.

a) Estimate the relative width of Cell A compared to Cell B.

....
[1]

b) Estimate the relative area of Cell A compared to Cell B.

....
[1]

[Total 2 marks]

2 A sample of epithelial cells were viewed using a light microscope.

The image on the right shows one of the cells.
A scale is included with the image.

a) Estimate the real height of the cell.

.... µm
[1]

b) Another sample of epithelial cells is viewed using an electron microscope.

Suggest **two** ways in which epithelial cells would look different when viewed with an electron microscope compared to when viewed with a light microscope.

1. ....

2. ....
[2]

[Total 3 marks]

PRACTICAL

3 The image on the right shows plant cells going through mitosis. The chromosomes in the image have been stained.

a) Explain why it is beneficial to stain the chromosomes.

....
....
[1]

b) Describe what is happening in the cell labelled **A**.

....
[1]

[Total 2 marks]

Chapter B4 — Using Food and Controlling Growth

More Microscopy

Warm-Up

Put the measurements below in order, from smallest to largest.

5 mm   4.9 nm   6 µm

....
smallest   largest

---

1 A student observed blood cells under a microscope.
A scale drawing of one of the cells is shown on the right.

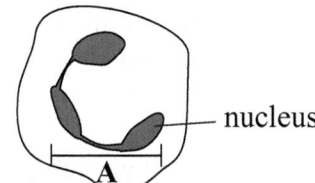

a) In the drawing, **A** is the width of the nucleus.
Measure the length of **A** with a ruler.

.... mm
[1]

b) The real width of the nucleus is 0.0075 mm.
Use your answer to part **a)** and the formula below to calculate the magnification of the cell in the drawing.

$$\text{magnification} = \frac{\text{measured size}}{\text{actual size}}$$

magnification = × ....
[1]

[Total 2 marks]

2 A plant cell is magnified 1000 times using a light microscope.

a) The length of the image of the plant cell is 10 mm.
Calculate the real length of one plant cell in millimetres (mm).
Use the formula:

$$\text{actual size} = \frac{\text{measured size}}{\text{magnification}}$$

.... mm
[1]

b) What is the real length of one plant cell in micrometres (µm)?

.... µm
[1]

[Total 2 marks]

Exam Practice Tip

Make sure you know how to convert one unit to another. To go from a bigger unit to a smaller unit (for example, from millimetres to micrometres) your calculation should be a <u>multiplication</u>. To go from a smaller unit to a bigger unit (e.g. from micrometres to millimetres) your calculation should be a <u>division</u>.

Chapter B4 — Using Food and Controlling Growth

Sexual Reproduction and Meiosis

1 Gametes are produced by meiosis. Human gametes are egg and sperm cells.

Which of the following statements about gametes is correct?
Place a tick (✓) in the box next to the correct answer.

Gametes contain twice as many chromosomes as other body cells. ☐

Gametes contain a quarter of the number of chromosomes in other body cells. ☐

Gametes contain three times as many chromosomes as other body cells. ☐

Gametes contain half the number of chromosomes in other body cells. ☐

[Total 1 mark]

2 The diagram on the right shows a cell about to undergo meiosis. It has made a copy of its DNA during interphase.

a) The cell goes through meiosis.
Which of the cells below shows the number of chromosomes that would be present in one of the daughter cells?
Place a tick (✓) in the box next to the correct answer.

A ☐ B ☐ C ☐ D ☐

[1]

b) How many cell divisions are there during the process of meiosis?

....

[1]

c) Briefly describe the results of meiosis.

....

....

....

....

[3]

[Total 5 marks]

Exam Practice Tip

It's pretty easy to get mitosis and meiosis mixed up because someone decided to give them such similar names. Remember, when you're talking about the production of gam<u>e</u>tes for sexual reproduction, it's m<u>e</u>iosis that you want.

Chapter B4 — Using Food and Controlling Growth

Stem Cells

1 Stem cells can be found in the growing areas of plants.

What are the growing areas of a plant that contain stem cells called?
Place a tick (✓) in the box next to the correct answer.

cloning zones ☐   meristems ☐   leaves ☐   stomata ☐

[Total 1 mark]

2 Stem cells can become specialised cells.

a) Look at the diagram below.

i) What is the name of the process marked **X** on the diagram?
Place a tick (✓) in the box next to the correct answer.

mutation ☐   adaptation ☐   functionalisation ☐   differentiation ☐
[1]

ii) What does a cell need to switch off and on in order to carry out the process marked **X** on the diagram?

....
[1]

b) Research scientists can use stem cells to produce a range of different cells, such as nerve cells, blood cells and heart cells.

i) Suggest why the scientists may prefer to use embryonic stem cells in their research rather than adult stem cells.

....

....

....
[2]

ii) Suggest **one** reason why some people are against research involving embryonic stem cells.

....
[1]

iii) What is the function of adult stem cells in the body?

....
[1]

[Total 6 marks]

Exchange of Materials

Warm-Up

Place the following organisms in order according to their surface area to volume ratio. Number the boxes 1 to 3, with 1 being the smallest and 3 being the largest.

☐ Tiger ☐ Bacterium ☐ Blue whale

1 Different substances are moved in and out of a human's blood. Which of the following statements is correct?
Put a tick (✓) in the box next to the correct answer.

Urea is absorbed into the blood by the small intestine. ☐

Water is absorbed into the blood by the lungs. ☐

Urea is filtered out of the blood by the kidneys. ☐

Oxygen is absorbed into the blood by the kidneys. ☐

[Total 1 mark]

2 Look at the diagram of a cube. The cube represents a small cell.

a) Which row in the table shows the correct surface area and volume of the cube?
Put a tick (✓) in the box next to the correct row.

Surface area (μm^2)	Volume (μm^3)
3	54
9	3
27	9
54	27

☐
☐
☐
☐
[1]

b) Another cell has a surface area of 24 μm^2. It has a volume of 8 μm^3.
What is its surface area to volume ratio? Put a tick (✓) in the box next to the correct answer.

3 : 1 ☐   2 : 1 ☐   1 : 3 ☐   1 : 2 ☐

[1]

c) The surface area to volume ratio of a cell affects how quickly it can take in the substances it needs. Give **three** substances an organism may need to take into its cells.

1. ....

2. ....

3. ....

[3]

[Total 5 marks]

Human Exchange Surfaces

1 A diagram of an alveolus and a capillary is shown below.

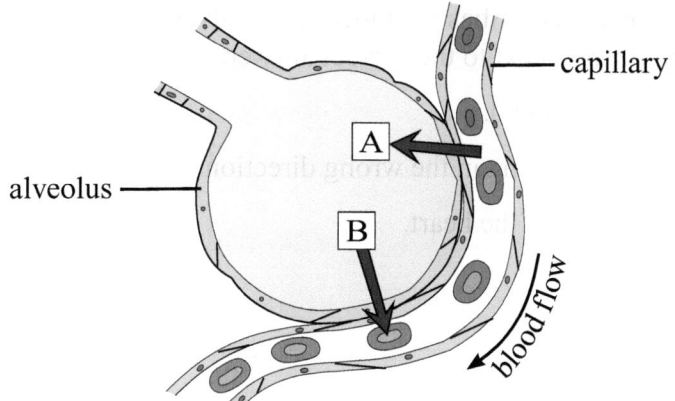

a) Name gases **A** and **B**.

  A ....

  B ....
  [2]

b) By what process do these gases move across the membrane of the alveolus?

  ....
  [1]
  [Total 3 marks]

2 The lining of the small intestine is covered in villi, as shown in the diagram below. Food molecules in the small intestine are absorbed across the surface of the villi.

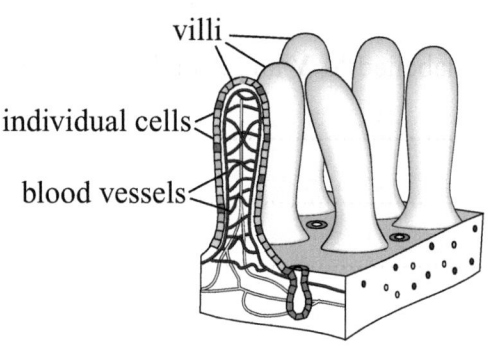

a) Explain how the shape of the villi affects the rate at which food molecules are absorbed.

  ....

  ....
  [2]

b) The villi have a good blood supply. Why is this important for their function?

  ....

  ....
  [1]
  [Total 3 marks]

Chapter B5 — The Human Body — Staying Alive

The Circulatory System

1 Valves are an important part of the heart's structure.

Which of the following describes the function of valves in the heart?
Put a tick (✓) in the box next to the correct answer.

They add oxygen to the blood. ☐

They stop blood from flowing in the wrong direction. ☐

They push the blood out of the heart. ☐

They make the heart beat. ☐

[Total 1 mark]

2 The diagram below shows the human heart.
The heart pumps blood around the body through a network of veins and arteries.

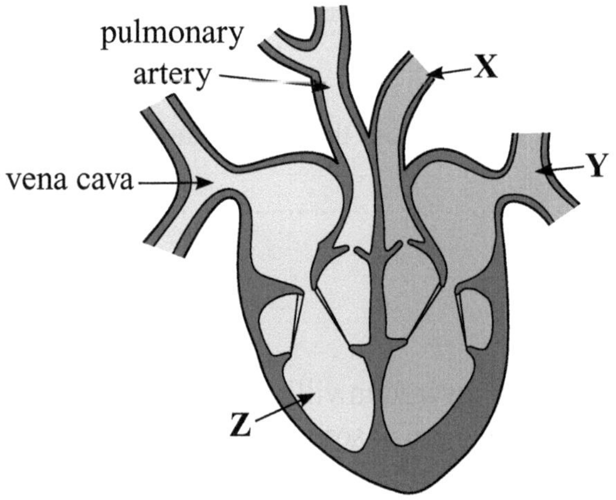

a) Name the parts of the heart labelled **X**, **Y** and **Z** in the diagram above.

X ....

Y ....

Z ....

[3]

b) The following steps describe how blood flows through the heart. Put the steps in order by writing the numbers **1** to **4** in the boxes. The first one has been done for you.

	Blood fills the right ventricle.
	Blood is pumped out of the atrium.
	Blood is pumped through the pulmonary artery.
1	Deoxygenated blood flows into the right atrium from the vena cava.

[1]

[Total 4 marks]

Chapter B5 — The Human Body — Staying Alive

Blood Vessels

Warm-Up

Draw a line to match each type of blood vessel on the left to its function on the right.

Vein — Carries blood away from the heart.

Artery — Carries blood towards the heart.

1 Different types of blood vessel have different structures.

Complete the table below to show whether each feature is part of a capillary, an artery or a vein. Put a tick (✓) in each row.

Feature	Capillary	Artery	Vein
Lots of elastic fibres in blood vessel walls			
Large lumen			
Walls that are one cell thick			
Valves			

[Total 3 marks]

2 The structure of blood vessels is related to their functions.

a) Describe the purpose of valves in a blood vessel.

....
[1]

b) Describe the function of capillaries.

....

....
[2]

c) Arteries have thick layers of muscle in their walls.
Explain why this is important for their function.

....

....

....
[2]

[Total 5 marks]

Blood

1 The function of a red blood cell is to carry a particular gas to cells in the body. The diagram below shows the shape of a red blood cell.

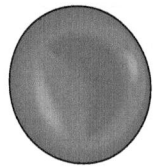 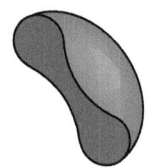

View from above   Cut through view

a) Name the gas that red blood cells carry to the body cells.

....
[1]

b) Describe how a red blood cell's shape helps it to carry out its function.

....
[1]

c) Red blood cells don't have a nucleus.
How does this help them to carry out their function?

....
[1]

d) Give **one** more feature of red blood cells that helps them to carry out their function.

....
[1]

[Total 4 marks]

2 Plasma makes up 55% of the total volume of blood.

a) What is the function of plasma?

....
[1]

b) An average adult human has 5000 cm³ of blood.
Calculate the volume of plasma in an average adult.

Answer = ... cm³
[2]

[Total 3 marks]

The Nervous System

Warm-Up

Complete the following passage about synapses using the words below.

receptors   axons   swim   transmitter   diffuse   effector

When a nervous impulse reaches a synapse, ... chemicals are released. They .... across the gap. These chemicals bind to .... in the membrane of the next neurone.

1 The nervous system allows communication between different parts of the body. Outline the pathway that nervous impulses take from a sensory receptor to an effector.

....
....
....

[Total 3 marks]

2 The diagram on the right shows a motor neurone.

a) Name the part labelled **X**.

....
[1]

b) Describe how the dendrites and axon help the motor neurone to carry out its function.

....
....
[2]

c) Explain why a person may not be able to respond to a stimulus if a motor neurone is damaged.

....
....
....
[2]

[Total 5 marks]

Reflexes

Warm-Up

Which of these actions is a reflex? Circle the correct answer.

Dropping a hot plate.   Writing a letter.   Running to catch a bus.

1   Mohini put her finger near a candle flame. She quickly moved her hand away from it. The diagram below shows the reflex arc involved in this movement.

a) i) Name structures **Y** and **Z**.

Y ....

Z ....
[2]

ii) Structure **A** is the junction between two neurones. Name structure **A**.

....
[1]

b) In the reflex arc shown in the diagram above, state:

the stimulus ....

the effector ....
[2]
[Total 5 marks]

2   Nervous impulses in reflex arcs go through the spinal cord or the unconscious part of the brain. This means that the part of the brain involved in thinking is **not** involved in a reflex arc. Suggest why this is a useful feature of reflexes.

....

....

....
[Total 2 marks]

Exam Practice Tip

The pathway that nervous impulses take in a reflex arc is always the same — from receptor to effector. Learn the full details of the pathway involved and you'll be able to tackle any question on reflexes, even if it's a reflex you've not learnt.

Chapter B5 — The Human Body — Staying Alive

Hormones in Reproduction

1 The endocrine system is a collection of glands in the body that secrete hormones.

a) Which of the following statements about glands is correct?
Put a tick (✓) in the box next to the correct answer.

Glands secrete hormones directly into cells. ☐
Glands secrete hormones directly into the blood. ☐
Glands secrete hormones directly into organs. ☐
Glands secrete hormones directly into tissues. ☐

[1]

b) Explain why a hormone will only cause a response from certain effectors within the body.

....

....
[1]

c) State **one** way in which communication by hormones differs from communication via the nervous system.

....
[1]

[Total 3 marks]

2 The diagram shows how the levels of two hormones change during the menstrual cycle.

Which line on the diagram, **X** or **Y**, represents progesterone? Explain your answer.

....

....

....

[Total 2 marks]

Chapter B5 — The Human Body — Staying Alive

Contraception

1 Condoms and the combined pill are two different methods of contraception.

a) How do condoms prevent pregnancy?
Put a tick (✓) in the box next to the correct answer.

They break down eggs once they have been fertilised by sperm. ☐

They prevent eggs from being released. ☐

They stop sperm from getting to an egg. ☐

They kill sperm. ☐

[1]

b) The combined pill contains hormones.
Suggest **one** hormone that the combined pill may contain and explain how the hormone would help to prevent pregnancy.

Hormone: ....

How it helps to prevent pregnancy: ....

....
[2]

c) Suggest **two** advantages of using condoms over the combined pill.

1. ....

2. ....
[2]

d) Suggest **two** disadvantages of using condoms over the combined pill.

1. ....

2. ....
[2]

[Total 7 marks]

2 With perfect use, for every 600 women who use male condoms as a method of contraception every time they have sex, an average of 12 will become pregnant over the course of a year.

Calculate how effective condoms are, with perfect use, as a percentage.

Answer = ... %

[Total 2 marks]

Homeostasis and Blood Sugar Level

1 The concentration of glucose in the blood is controlled by hormones.

a) Which gland in the human body monitors and controls blood glucose concentration?

....
[1]

b) Which hormone is produced when blood glucose concentration becomes too high?

....
[1]

c) Use words from the box to complete the sentences below.

| pancreas | glycogen | insulin | liver | protein |

When there is too much glucose in the blood, some of it moves into the ....

The glucose is then changed into .... so it can be stored.

[2]

[Total 4 marks]

2 Diabetes exists in two different forms, type 1 and type 2.

a) Which of these describes **type 1** diabetes?
Put a tick (✓) in the box next to the correct answer.

The body stops making glucose. ☐

The body doesn't respond properly to its own insulin. ☐

The body makes too much insulin. ☐

The body stops making insulin. ☐

[1]

b) What can happen if diabetes is left untreated?

....
[1]

c) How is **type 1** diabetes treated?

....
[1]

d) Give **two** treatments that a doctor may recommend for **type 2** diabetes.

1. ....

2. ....

[2]

[Total 5 marks]

Chapter B6 — Life on Earth — Past, Present and Future

Natural Selection and Evolution

Warm-Up

Place a tick (✓) in the box next to the correct sentence about evolution and natural selection.

Evolution is the change in the inherited characteristics of a population over several generations, through the process of natural selection. ☐

Natural selection is the change in the inherited characteristics of a population over several generations, through the process of evolution. ☐

1 Most populations of organisms have a lot of genetic variation.

Which of the following statements is **true**?
Place a tick (✓) in the box next to the correct answer.

Most genetic variants have no effect on the characteristics of an organism. ☐

All genetic variants affect the characteristics of an organism. ☐

Most genetic variants have a large effect on the characteristics of an organism. ☐

Genetic variants never have an effect on the characteristics of an organism. ☐

[Total 1 mark]

2* The photograph on the right is of a hare species which lives in a warm climate. It has large ears which help to keep it cool. The size of ears in hares is partly controlled by genes.

Describe how natural selection could have led to the evolution of hares with large ears, from a population of hares with smaller ears.

....

....

....

....

....

....

....

....

....

[Total 6 marks]

Evidence for Evolution

1 Bacteria can evolve to become resistant to antibiotics.

What is the process by which a population of bacteria can become resistant to antibiotics?
Place a tick (✓) in the box next to the correct answer.

normal variation ☐   natural selection ☐   natural variation ☐   normal selection ☐

[Total 1 mark]

2 The diagram below shows fossils of feet from species that modern humans have evolved from (Fossil **A** and Fossil **B**). It also shows the bones of a modern human foot.

Fossil A   Fossil B   Modern human foot

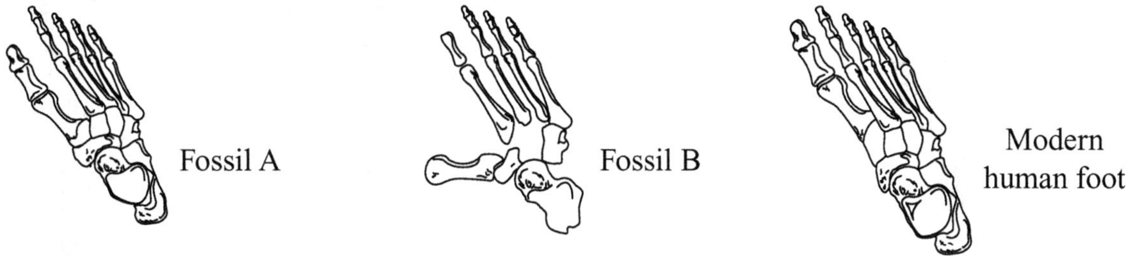

Fossil **A** is thought to be more recent than Fossil **B**.
Suggest why scientists think this from looking at the fossils.

....

....

[Total 1 mark]

3 A patient with a bacterial infection was treated with an antibiotic. The diagram below represents the bacteria present at the site of infection before, during and after treatment. There are two different types of bacterial cell present, '**A**' and '**B**'. '**A**' have a genetic variant that makes them resistant to the antibiotic the patient is being treated with.

Before treatment with the antibiotic.   One week after starting treatment with the antibiotic.   Two weeks after starting treatment with the antibiotic.

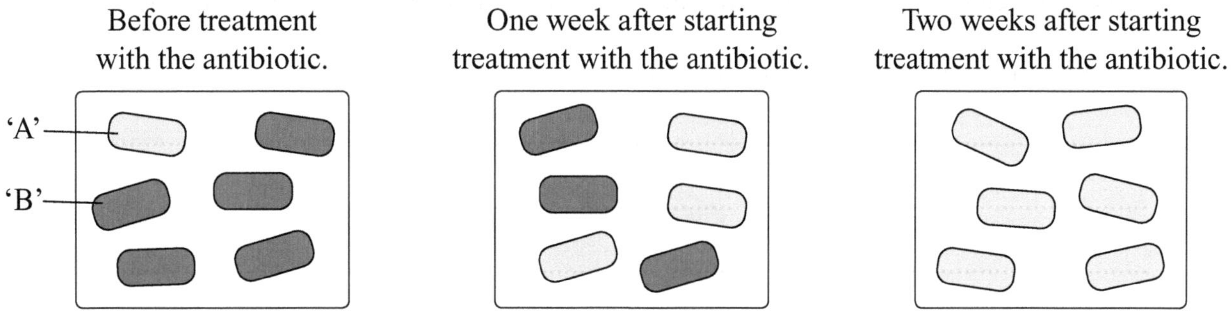

Explain why there are more '**A**' bacterial cells present two weeks after starting treatment than before the treatment started.

....

....

....

[Total 3 marks]

Chapter B6 — Life on Earth — Past, Present and Future

Selective Breeding

1 Selective breeding is used in several different industries.

a) What is selective breeding?

....
[1]

b) Four wheat plants (**A-D**) are shown below. Each plant has different characteristics.

Which **two** plants should be bred together to get a wheat plant with a tall stem and a large head?

....
[1]

c) State **two** problems that can be caused by selective breeding.

1. ....

2. ....
[2]
[Total 4 marks]

2 Selective breeding can be used to produce farm animals with certain characteristics.

Describe the process used in selective breeding.

....

....

....

....

....
[Total 3 marks]

Exam Practice Tip

Make sure you understand how selective breeding works, as it could come up in the exams. You could be asked to describe the process of selective breeding in a context that you haven't come across before. You don't need to worry though — as long as you know what the basic process is, you can apply it to any example that comes up.

Classification

Warm-Up

What is classification? Circle the correct answer below to complete the sentence.

Classification means...

...finding the total number of different organisms on Earth.

...putting different types of organisms into age order.

...sorting organisms into groups.

1 Evolutionary trees show how scientists think organisms are related to each other. The diagram on the right shows the evolutionary tree for species **A-G**.

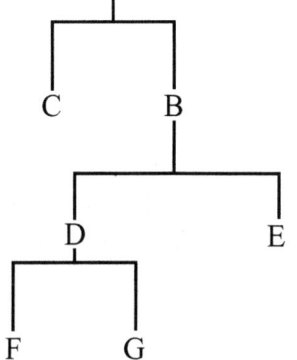

a) Which species is the most distant ancestor of species **F**?

....
[1]

b) Which species is the most common recent ancestor of species **D** and **E**?

....
[1]

[Total 2 marks]

2 DNA analysis can be used to classify organisms.

a) Describe **one** way in which scientists classified organisms before it was possible to use methods such as DNA analysis.

....

....
[1]

b) Describe how scientists use the DNA of organisms to classify them into groups.

....

....

....
[2]

c) Give **one** advantage of using DNA analysis over other methods for classifying organisms.

....

....
[1]

[Total 4 marks]

Chapter B6 — Life on Earth — Past, Present and Future

Biodiversity

Warm-Up

Circle the correct underlined word to complete each sentence below.

If the number of species in an area decreases, biodiversity in the area increases / **decreases**.

Human activities that damage ecosystems are likely to increase / **decrease** biodiversity.

1 Humans need natural resources in order to survive. By using resources sustainably humans can protect the resources they need as well as protecting biodiversity. *(Grade 3-4)*

a) Explain what it means if resources are used sustainably.

....

....
[1]

b) Which of the statements below could be used to complete the following sentence?
Biodiversity is the variety of .... in an area.
Place a tick (✓) in the box next to **two** correct answers.

living organisms ☐   genes and alleles ☐

rainfall patterns ☐   temperature ranges ☐

[2]
[Total 3 marks]

2 In the UK, many areas of woodland have been cut down so that the land can be used for other things. *(Grade 4-5)*

a) Suggest **two** things that humans might want to use the land for.

1. ....

2. ....
[2]

b) Describe the effect that cutting down areas of woodland has on the biodiversity of **plant** species.

....
[1]

c) Suggest how cutting down areas of woodland is likely to affect the biodiversity of **animal** species in the area. Explain your answer.

....

....

....
[2]
[Total 5 marks]

Chapter B6 — Life on Earth — Past, Present and Future

3 The ecosystem in which a species lives can change over time. A species can gradually adapt so that it can survive these changes.

Grade 4-5

a) Some human activities are causing ecosystems to change very quickly.
Explain why these human activities can lead to the extinction of some species.

....

....
[1]

b) The human population is rising very quickly.
Explain why a rising human population may cause ecosystems to change more quickly.

....

....
[1]

c) Explain **one** way in which humans can help to protect ecosystems from change.

....

....
[1]

[Total 3 marks]

4 Globalisation results in countries sharing their resources. For example, the Cavendish banana is a variety of banana. It was bred from bananas from Mauritius, an island off the coast of East Africa. It is now grown in many countries around the world.

Grade 4-5

a) Suggest how growing the Cavendish banana in many countries may reduce the biodiversity of banana plants.

....

....
[1]

b) In some countries, aeroplanes are used to spray banana plants with pesticides. These are chemicals used to kill pests, such as insects.

Suggest what effect spraying pesticides will have on biodiversity in areas where bananas are grown. Explain your answer.

....

....

....
[2]

[Total 3 marks]

Chapter B6 — Life on Earth — Past, Present and Future

Maintaining Biodiversity

1 Which of the following statements about maintaining biodiversity is **false**?
Place a tick (✓) in the box next to the correct answer.

Protecting one species can help to protect other species. ☐

Maintaining biodiversity can help to provide humans with materials. ☐

People never argue against schemes that aim to protect a species. ☐

Maintaining biodiversity can help to provide humans with food. ☐

[Total 1 mark]

2 Kruger National Park is a large national park in South Africa.

a) Give **one** potential advantage to **medicine** of protected areas such as Kruger National Park.

....

....
[1]

b) Suggest **one economic reason** why some people may disagree with conservation schemes such as Kruger National Park.

....

....
[1]

[Total 2 marks]

3 Overfishing has reduced the number of bluefin tuna in the world.
Bluefin tuna travel through waters that many different countries use for harvesting fish.

a) Give **one** reason why controlling the fishing of bluefin tuna may be beneficial to humans.

....
[1]

b) Suggest **one** political difficulty in setting up a scheme to limit the amount of bluefin tuna that can be caught.

....

....
[1]

[Total 2 marks]

Exam Practice Tip

You should know about the positive effects maintaining biodiversity can have on ecosystems and the benefits it can have for humans. But maintaining biodiversity isn't always easy — make sure you're aware of some of the challenges involved.

Chapter B6 — Life on Earth — Past, Present and Future

Chapter C1 — Air and Water

States of Matter

Warm-Up

The diagrams below show how the particles are arranged in different states of matter. Below each diagram, write the name of the state of matter (solid, liquid or gas) that it shows.

....

---

1 Substances exist in one of the three states of matter — solid, liquid or gas.

a) Place solids, liquids and gases in order of the strength of attraction between their particles.

Strongest attraction   ....

                           ....

Weakest attraction   ....

[1]

b) When gases and liquids are placed inside a container they change shape. Explain why this does **not** happen when a solid is put inside a container.

....

....

[2]

[Total 3 marks]

---

2 When a substance changes state, this is known as a physical change. When a substance reacts with another substance, a chemical change happens.

Describe the difference between a physical change and a chemical change. Give your answer in terms of the end product.

....

....

....

[Total 2 marks]

Changing State

1 This question is about changing state.

The arrows in the diagram represent processes that cause a change in state to happen.

```
[Solid] ←――A――― [Liquid]
        ――B――→
```

a) Process **A** causes a liquid to turn into a solid. Name this process.

....

[1]

b) Process **B** causes a solid to turn into a liquid. Name this process.

....

[1]
[Total 2 marks]

2 Hexane is a hydrocarbon with a boiling point of 69 °C.
A scientist carefully heats a sample of liquid hexane from 50 °C to 69 °C.
Describe what happens to the particles in the hexane as it is heated.

....

....

....

....

[Total 3 marks]

3 The melting and boiling points of three substances are shown in the table below.

Substance	Sodium Chloride	Water	Copper
Melting Point (°C)	801	0	1083
Boiling Point (°C)	1413	100	2560

a) Which substance in the table would be a liquid at 900 °C?

....

[1]

b) Which **two** substances in the table would be gases at 1500 °C?

....

[2]
[Total 3 marks]

Chapter C1 — Air and Water

Chemical Formulas

Warm-Up

Using a periodic table, write the symbols of the following elements.

Boron: ....   Tin: ....   Iron: ....   Chlorine: ....

1 Propanol is commonly used as a solvent.
The diagram below shows the displayed formula for a propanol molecule.

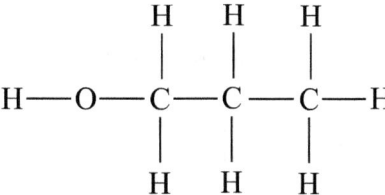

a) What do the lines between the atoms represent?

....
[1]

b) How many hydrogen atoms are there in a molecule of propanol?

....
[1]
[Total 2 marks]

2 The chemical formulas of three different substances, **A**, **B** and **C** are shown below.

A O_2 **B** $CH_2(OH)_2$ **C** $C_6H_4(NH_2)_2$

a) How many elements are there in a molecule of substance **A**?

....
[1]

b) How many atoms are there altogether in one molecule of substance **B**?

....
[1]

c) State how many atoms of carbon, nitrogen and hydrogen are in one molecule of substance **C**.

carbon: ....   nitrogen: ....   hydrogen: ....
[2]
[Total 4 marks]

Exam Practice Tip
Don't panic if you're asked a question about a chemical formula that has brackets in it. Take it chunk by chunk. Start by writing down how many atoms are outside the brackets, then work out how many atoms are inside the brackets.

Chapter C1 — Air and Water

Chemical Equations

Warm-Up

The word equation for a reaction is shown below:

magnesium + hydrochloric acid → magnesium chloride + hydrogen

For each of the following statements circle whether the statement is **true** or **false**.

1) Hydrogen is a product of the reaction.   True   Or   False

2) The equation shows the reaction between chlorine and hydrogen.   True   Or   False

3) Hydrochloric acid is a reactant in this reaction.   True   Or   False

4) The equation shows the reaction between magnesium and hydrochloric acid.   True   Or   False

---

1 Iron (III) oxide, Fe_2O_3, is produced in a reaction between iron and oxygen.

a) Write a word equation for this reaction.

....
[1]

b) Which of the following is the correct balanced symbol equation for this reaction? Place a tick (✓) in the box next to the correct answer.

$2Fe + 3O_2 \rightarrow Fe_2O_3$ ☐

$4Fe + 3O_2 \rightarrow 2Fe_2O_3$ ☐

$3Fe + 3O_2 \rightarrow 3Fe_2O_3$ ☐

$2Fe + 3O_2 \rightarrow 2Fe_2O_3$ ☐

[1]
[Total 1 mark]

---

2 Sodium (Na) reacts with chlorine gas (Cl_2) to form sodium chloride (NaCl) only.

a) Balance the equation for this reaction. You may not need to put numbers on every line.

.... Na + ... Cl_2 → .... NaCl

[2]

b) Sodium also reacts with oxygen (O_2) to form sodium oxide (Na_2O). Write a balanced symbol equation for this reaction.

....
[2]
[Total 4 marks]

Chapter C1 — Air and Water

Endothermic and Exothermic Reactions

1 The diagram below shows the energy profile of a reaction.

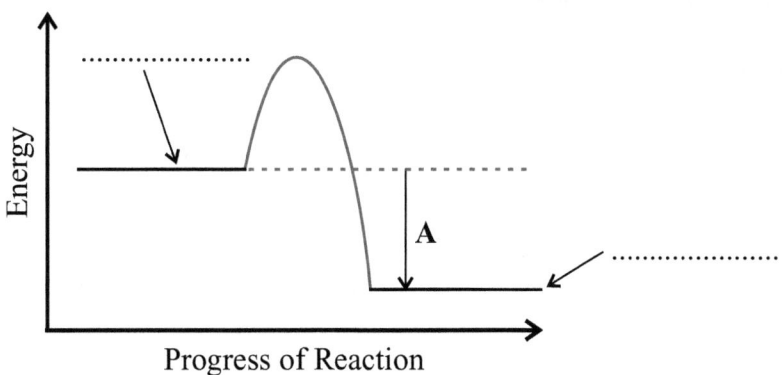

a) Complete the two missing labels in the diagram.

[2]

b) **A** shows an energy change.
What does this energy change represent?

....

[1]

[Total 3 marks]

2 During a reaction between a solution of citric acid and a solution of sodium hydrogen carbonate, the temperature fell from 22 °C to 15 °C.

a) Is this reaction exothermic or endothermic? Give a reason for your answer.

....

....

[2]

b) In this reaction, the products are at a higher energy than the reactants.
Sketch a reaction profile for this reaction on the axes below.
Label the reactants and products.

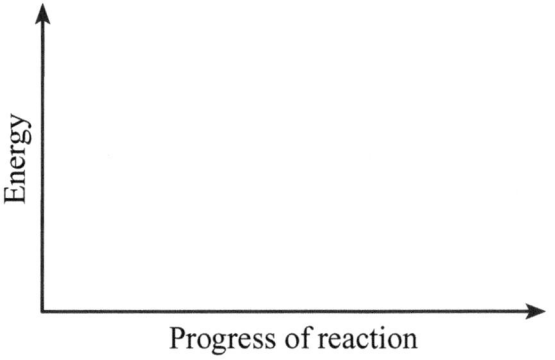

[2]

[Total 4 marks]

Chapter C1 — Air and Water

Bond Energies

1 For a reaction to happen, particles need to collide with enough energy.

a) Define the term 'activation energy'.

....

[1]

b) The diagram below shows the reaction profile of a reaction.

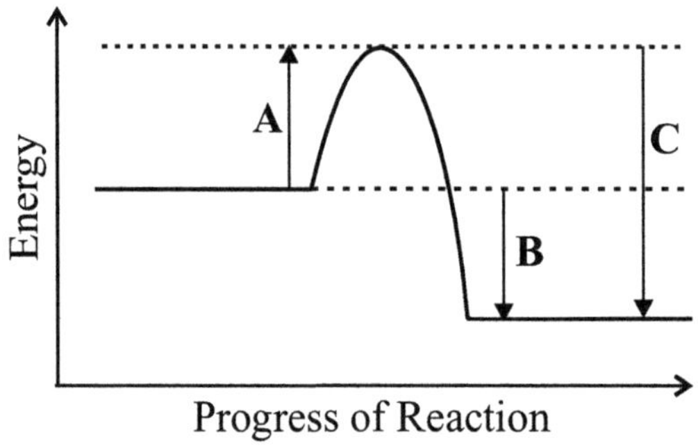

Which letter, **A**, **B**, or **C** shows the activation energy of this reaction?

....

[1]

[Total 2 marks]

2 Dylan carried out a computer simulation of two exothermic reactions, **A** and **B**. The computer programme created reaction profiles for both of the reactions, which are shown below. The reaction profiles are both drawn on the same scale.

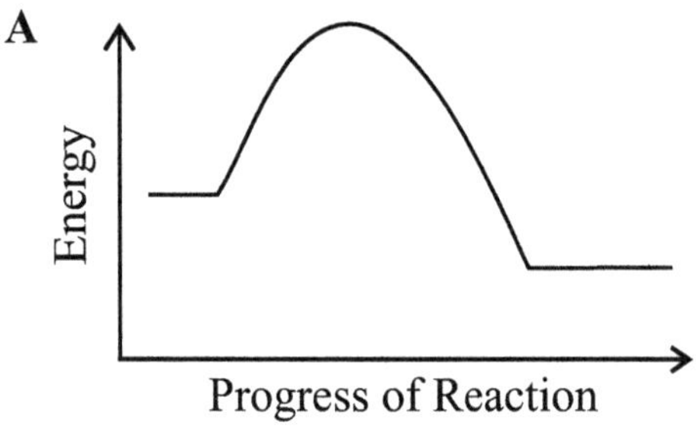

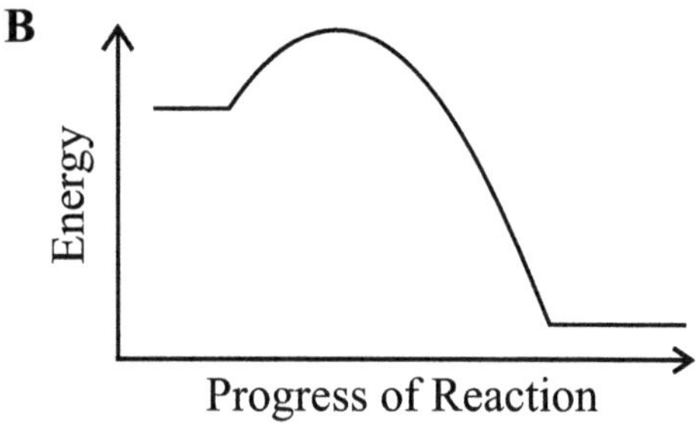

a) State which reaction has the greatest overall energy change. Explain how you can tell.

....

....

[2]

b) During reaction **A**, is more energy used to break the bonds in the reactants or given out when the bonds in the products form? Give a reason for your answer.

....

....

[2]

[Total 4 marks]

The Evolution of the Atmosphere

Warm-Up

Write the numbers 1-4 in the boxes below to put these events in order.

Oxygen levels in Earth's atmosphere began to rise. ☐   Earth's oceans formed. ☐

Earth's early atmosphere formed. ☐   Plants evolved. ☐

1   The mixture of gases that make up the atmosphere has varied during Earth's history.

a) How was the oxygen that is present in our atmosphere today produced?

....
[1]

b) The early Earth was much hotter than today.
Describe what happened to the water vapour in the atmosphere as the Earth cooled.

....
[1]

[Total 2 marks]

2*   The table below shows some information about two fossils.

Age (years)	Description
950 000 000	Fossils of some bacteria that can survive in high levels of CO_2.
295 000 000	Fossil of a lizard that can survive in high levels of O_2 and low levels of CO_2.

Describe how the amount of carbon dioxide in the atmosphere got to the level that it is at today.
Include ideas about:
- How carbon dioxide originally became part of the atmosphere.
- How the amount of carbon dioxide in the early atmosphere was different to how it is today.
- Reasons why the amount of atmospheric carbon dioxide has changed.
- Whether the information in the table supports your answer.

....
....
....
....
....
....
....

[Total 6 marks]

Chapter C1 — Air and Water

Combustion and Greenhouse Gases

1 When hydrocarbon fuels are burned in plenty of oxygen, complete combustion occurs. But in low levels of oxygen, incomplete combustion occurs instead

a) The word equation for the complete combustion of a hydrocarbon is shown below.

hydrocarbon + oxygen → carbon dioxide + water

Explain why the carbon and hydrogen can be said to have been oxidised.

....
[1]

b) Incomplete combustion produces tiny particles of carbon.
Name **one** health problem that may be caused by these particles.

....
[1]

c) Combustion of fuels can also produce a toxic gas that can stop oxygen being delivered to cells.
Name this gas and explain how it stops oxygen from being delivered to cells.

....

....

....
[3]
[Total 5 marks]

2 Electromagnetic radiation from the Sun passes through Earth's atmosphere.
The Earth absorbs some of this radiation, warming it up.
It then radiates out some of the energy that it has absorbed.

a) What type of radiation is given out by the Earth during this process?

....
[1]

b) Some of the radiation given out by the Earth is absorbed by greenhouse gases.

i) Name **two** greenhouses gases.

1. ....

2. ....
[2]

ii) Describe what happens to the radiation absorbed by the greenhouse gases.

....
[1]
[Total 4 marks]

Climate Change

1 Over the last hundred years, the average global temperature of planet Earth has increased. It is currently still increasing.

a) Give **two** examples of types of climate change that could be caused by increasing global temperatures.

1. ....

2. ....
[2]

b) Give **one** possible reason for the change in temperature.

....
[1]
[Total 3 marks]

2 The graph below shows how the carbon dioxide concentration in the Earth's atmosphere has changed since 1900.

a) Describe what the graph tells you about the level of carbon dioxide in the Earth's atmosphere.

....
[1]

b) Burning fossil fuels produces carbon dioxide.

i) Predict what would happen to the level of carbon dioxide in the atmosphere if there was an increase in the amount of fossil fuels being used.

....
[1]

ii) Suggest **one** other human activity that can affect the level of carbon dioxide in the atmosphere.

....
[1]

c) Suggest **one** thing scientists could do to increase confidence in their predictions about the climate.

....
[1]
[Total 4 marks]

Reducing Greenhouse Gas Emissions

1. Governments can take action to try to reduce the greenhouse gas emissions of whole countries. Individual companies can also take actions to reduce their own greenhouse gas emissions.

   Place a tick (✓) in each row of the table below to show the best scale of organisation for carrying out each of these actions to reduce greenhouse gas emissions. The first row has been completed for you.

Action	Company	Government
Putting a tax on lightbulbs that use lots of energy		✓
Running a car share scheme for getting to work.		
Funding research into renewable energy sources.		
Printing all documents on recycled paper.		
Taxing cars based on how much fuel they use.		

   [Total 2 marks]

2. A company is investigating methods to reduce its carbon dioxide emissions.

   a) Some companies invest in tree-planting schemes to help reduce the amount of carbon dioxide in the atmosphere. Explain how planting trees could help to do this.

   ....
   [1]

   b) The company decides to invest in a carbon capture scheme.

   i) Describe how a carbon capture scheme reduces the level of carbon dioxide in the atmosphere.

   ....

   ....
   [2]

   ii) Give **two** disadvantages of using carbon capture schemes.

   1. ....

   2. ....
   [2]
   [Total 5 marks]

Exam Practice Tip

In the exam you might get asked to think about ways that companies, governments or individuals could limit their carbon dioxide emissions. It's not an easy thing to tackle, because the scale of the problem is so big. And we need to be careful what we do, because any changes we make could have impacts in the future that we didn't predict.

Chapter C1 — Air and Water

Pollutants and Tests for Gases

1   Amelia carries out an experiment that produces a gas.
    She collects the gas and tests it to find out if it is chlorine.

    The diagram below shows chlorine gas being tested.

    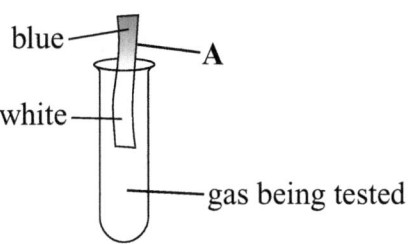

    a) Identify the item labelled **A** in the diagram.

    ....
    [1]

    b) How can you tell from the diagram that chlorine gas was present?

    ....
    [1]
    [Total 2 marks]

2   A power station burns fossil fuels to produce energy.
    The power station produces large amounts of the pollutant gas sulfur dioxide.

    a) Explain how sulfur dioxide is formed when fossil fuels are burned.

    ....

    ....
    [2]

    b) Sulfur dioxide and nitrogen oxides can cause acid rain.

       i) Describe **one** way that acid rain can damage the environment.

       ....
       [1]

       ii) Name **one** other environmental problem caused by sulfur dioxide and nitrogen oxides.

       ....
       [1]

    c) Give **two** ways that the power station could reduce its emissions of sulfur dioxide.

       1. ....

       2. ....
       [2]
       [Total 6 marks]

Chapter C1 — Air and Water

Water Treatment

1 Different places have different sources of water. The method used to treat the water depends on the source it has come from.

a) Draw lines to match each water source with its correct description.

Ground water		Water from the sea
Salt water		Water polluted by a human process
Waste water		Water found trapped in rocks underground

[2]

b) Aeration is a process used in water treatment.
Use words from the box to complete the following sentences about aeration.

| solid | oxygen | dissolved | minerals | air | chlorine |

Aeration is a process where water is mixed with ....,

in order to increase the levels of .... in the water.

This also forces other .... gases that could be harmful out of the water.

[3]

[Total 5 marks]

2 The treatment of waste water involves many stages.

a) Explain why treating waste water involves more stages than treating ground water.

....

[1]

b) Waste water is often filtered to make it potable.
What is the purpose of filtration? Draw a circle around the correct answer.

    removing bacteria   removing solid impurities   removing salt   removing oxygen

[1]

c) Treating waste water usually costs more than treating ground water. Give **one** example of a situation where a country might choose to treat and use waste water instead of ground water.

....

[1]

[Total 3 marks]

Chapter C1 — Air and Water

3 Kate and Gary are talking about the advantages and disadvantages of chlorinating water.

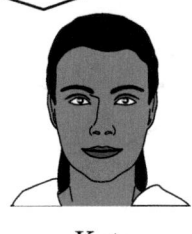
Kate: Chlorination is a good thing, because it makes water safer to drink.

Gary: Yes, but there are too many risks involved. Water should not be chlorinated.

a) Suggest **one** reason that supports Kate's statement and **one** reason that supports Gary's statement.

Kate: ....

Gary: ....

[2]

b) Governments often make sure that drinking water is chlorinated.
What effect would there be on human health if this was not the case?

....

[1]

[Total 3 marks]

4 Australia has a low annual rainfall. It produces some of its drinking water from filtering salt water using membranes.

a) Which of the following statements describes how membranes help to purify salt water?
Place a tick (✓) in the box next to the correct answer.

The membranes let salt molecules pass through but trap the water molecules. ☐

The membranes let water molecules pass through but trap the salts. ☐

The membranes do not let either the salts or the water molecules pass through. ☐

The membranes heat the water causing it to evaporate. ☐

[1]

b) Treating salt water using membranes can be carried out on a large scale.
Suggest **one** disadvantage of using membranes to treat salt water.

....

[1]

c) Drinking water can also be produced from salt water using distillation.
Briefly describe how distillation can be used to obtain pure water from salt water.

....

....

....

[3]

[Total 5 marks]

Chapter C2 — Chemical Patterns

The History of the Atom

Warm-Up

Use the words below to label the different parts of the atom shown on the right.

shell   electron   nucleus

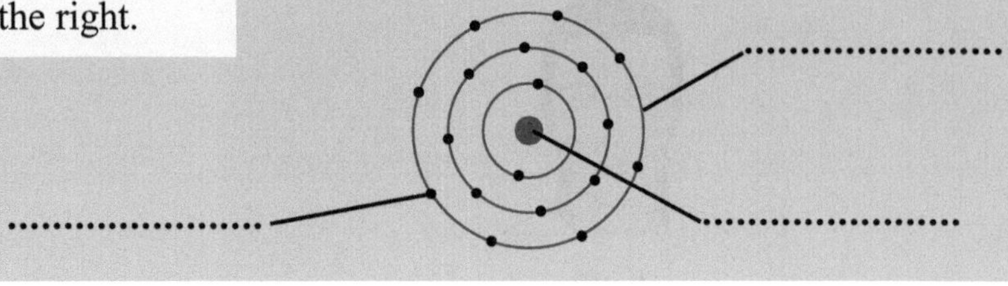

---

1 Models of the atom have changed over time. *(Grade 3-4)*

a) Which of the following is the best description of what scientists like Dalton thought atoms were like before the electron was discovered?
Place a tick (✓) in the box next to the correct answer.

Solid spheres ☐   Formless 'clouds' ☐   Flat shapes ☐   Packets of energy ☐

[1]

b) Look at the model of the atom shown in the diagram on the right.
Give the name of this model and the name of the scientist who developed it.

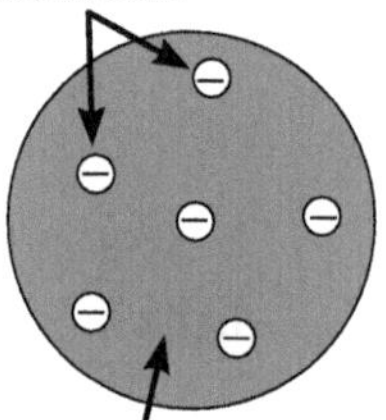

....

....

[2]

[Total 3 marks]

---

2 A scientist called Rutherford carried out an experiment where he fired positively charged alpha particles at a thin sheet of gold. *(Grade 4-5)*

a) The experiment gave an unexpected result.
Place a tick (✓) in the box next to the statement that best describes the result of the experiment.

All of the alpha particles passed through the sheet of gold without changing direction. ☐

The sheet of gold was destroyed by the alpha particles. ☐

Some alpha particles changed direction by more than Rutherford expected. ☐

The alpha particles could not pass through the sheet of gold. ☐

[1]

b) The results of Rutherford's experiment led him to create a new model of the atom.
Describe **two** differences between this new model and the one that came before it.

1. ....

2. ....

[2]

[Total 3 marks]

The Atom

1 Atoms are made up of different particles.

a) Use words from the box to complete the following sentences about atoms.

| protons | molecules | neutrons | electrons | bonds |

.... and .... are found in the nucleus of an atom.

The .... in an atom move around the nucleus in shells.

[3]

b) The relative charge of a proton is 1.

i) What is the relative charge of an electron?

....
[1]

ii) What is the relative charge of a neutron?

....
[1]

[Total 4 marks]

2 An oxygen atom has a diameter of approximately 1×10^{-10} m.
A single molecule of glucose is roughly ten times bigger than an atom of oxygen.
What is the approximate diameter, in metres, of a single molecule of glucose?
Place a tick (✓) in the box next to the correct answer.

1×10^1 m ☐

1×10^{10} m ☐

1×10^{-9} m ☐

1×10^{-11} m ☐

[Total 1 mark]

3 Most of the mass of any atom is found in its nucleus.
Use the relative masses of the subatomic particles to explain why.

....

....

....
[Total 2 marks]

Chapter C2 — Chemical Patterns

Atoms and Isotopes

1 A potassium atom can be represented by the nuclear symbol $^{39}_{19}K$.

a) State the mass number and atomic number of $^{39}_{19}K$.

mass number: ....

atomic number: ....
[2]

b) How many protons, neutrons and electrons does an atom of $^{39}_{19}K$ have?

protons: ....

neutrons: ....

electrons: ....
[3]
[Total 5 marks]

2 Isotopes are different forms of the same element.

a) Bromine has two stable isotopes, A and B. The table shows some information about them. Complete the table by calculating the number of neutrons and electrons for each isotope.

isotope	mass number	number of protons	number of neutrons	number of electrons
A	79	35	....	....
B	81	35	....	....

[2]

b) The nuclear symbols for two atoms are shown below.

$$^{54}_{26}X \qquad ^{54}_{24}Y$$

Are the atoms isotopes? Give a reason for your answer.

....

....

....
[2]
[Total 4 marks]

Exam Practice Tip

Don't let isotopes confuse you. Just because they've got different numbers of neutrons, a pair of isotopes will still have the same number of protons. This means they have the same atomic number but different mass numbers. Simple.

Chapter C2 — Chemical Patterns

The Periodic Table

1 The periodic table shows all the elements that have been discovered so far.

a) By which property are the elements in the periodic table ordered?
Place a tick (✓) in the box next to the correct answer.

boiling point ☐

atomic number ☐

number of neutrons ☐

atomic mass ☐

[1]

b) A element is in Group 7 of the periodic table.
How many electrons will it have in its outer shell?
Draw a circle around the correct answer.

      1   4   7   0

[1]
[Total 2 marks]

2 Dmitri Mendeleev made one of the first periodic tables.

a) Mendeleev arranged the elements in vertical columns.
What did the elements in the same vertical column have in common?

....

[1]

b) What is the name given to the rows in Mendeleev's periodic table?

....

[1]

c) Mendeleev thought that there were elements still to be discovered.
How did he take this into account?

....

[1]

d) Scientists later discovered many new elements.
How did these discoveries support Mendeleev's ideas about the periodic table?

....

....

[1]
[Total 4 marks]

Electronic Structure

1 Complete the table below to show how many electrons go in the first three electron shells.

Electron shell	Number of electrons it can hold
1st	....
2nd	....
3rd	....

[Total 3 marks]

2 Argon has an atomic number of 18.

a) What is the electronic structure of an argon atom?
Place a tick (✓) in the box next to the correct answer.

2, 16 ☐   2, 14, 2 ☐   2, 8, 8 ☐   8, 8, 2 ☐

[1]

b) Which shells do electrons fill first in an atom?

....
[1]
[Total 2 marks]

3 The elements aluminium and sulfur are both in Period 3 of the Periodic Table.

a) An atom of aluminium (Al) contains 13 electrons.
Write out the electronic structure of aluminium.

....
[1]

b) Sulfur has an atomic number of 16.
Complete the diagram below to show the electronic structure of sulfur.

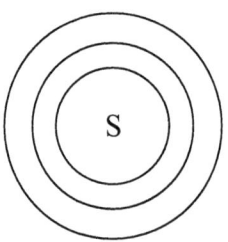

[2]
[Total 3 marks]

Exam Practice Tip

Make sure that you can remember how many electrons fit in each of the first three electron shells in an atom.
That way you'll be able to work out the electronic structure of any of the early elements in the periodic table.

Chapter C2 — Chemical Patterns

Metals and Non-Metals

1 About 80% of all the elements in the periodic table are metals.

a) Describe where metals can be found in the periodic table.

....
[1]

b) Which **two** of the following properties are typical properties of metals?
Place ticks (✓) in the boxes next to the **two** correct answers.

Conductors of electricity ☐

Liquids at room temperature ☐

Can be bent or hammered into different shapes ☐

Low density ☐

[2]
[Total 3 marks]

2 Some metals will react with particular non-metals to form compounds made of ions.

a) Two elements, with the chemical symbols A and X, react together to form a compound.
The compound is made up of A^{2+} ions and X^{2-} ions.
State whether each element is a metal or a non-metal.

Element A: ....

Element X: ....
[1]

b) Use words from the box to complete the following sentences about how metals react.

| gain | lose | share | half full | full |

When metals react, they .... electrons.

When this happens they generally end up with a .... outer shell of electrons.
[2]

c) State **three** physical properties that non-metals are likely to have.

1. ....

2. ....

3. ....
[3]
[Total 6 marks]

Chapter C2 — Chemical Patterns

Group 1 Elements and Their Reactions

Warm-Up

Place a tick (✓) in the correct box next to each of the statements.

Statement	True	False
Group 1 elements are non-metals.		
Group 1 elements are reactive.		
All Group 1 atoms are the same size.		
Group 1 elements react in similar ways.		

1 The Group 1 elements show trends in their properties.

a) The reactivity of the Group 1 elements **increases** down the group. Put the elements sodium (Na), lithium (Li) and potassium (K) in order from least reactive to most reactive.

.... Least reactive

....

.... Most reactive

[1]

b) State how the melting points of the elements in Group 1 change as you move down the group.

....

[1]

[Total 2 marks]

2 A scientist reacts a small piece of lithium with some chlorine.

a) What is the charge on the lithium ions that form in this reaction?

....

[1]

b) The scientist carries out the reaction again, but using sodium instead of lithium. How would this affect the rate of the reaction?

....

[1]

[Total 2 marks]

Chapter C2 — Chemical Patterns

3 Sodium is usually stored in oil, because it reacts with moist air. A teacher shows this reaction to her students. She takes a small piece of sodium out of oil, cuts it in half and leaves it open to the air for a few minutes. A new substance forms on the cut surface.

a) What substance in the air has the sodium reacted with?

....
[1]

b) Name the new substance that has formed on the cut surface of the sodium.

....
[1]

c) Describe how the appearance of the cut surface would change during this experiment.

....

....
[1]
[Total 3 marks]

4 Rubidium is a metal that is found in Group 1 of the periodic table. It reacts with water to form the alkali RuOH and hydrogen gas.

a) Give the name of the compound RuOH.

....
[1]

b) Which of these is the correct balanced symbol equation for this reaction?
Place a tick (✓) in the box next to the correct answer.

$2Ru_{(s)} + 2H_2O_{(l)} \rightarrow 2RuOH_{(aq)} + H_{2(g)}$ ☐

$2Ru_{(s)} + 2H_2O_{(l)} \rightarrow 2RuOH_{(aq)} + O_{2(g)}$ ☐

$Ru_{(s)} + H_2O_{(l)} \rightarrow RuOH_{(aq)} + 2H_2O_{(l)}$ ☐

$Ru_{(s)} + H_2O_{(l)} \rightarrow RuOH_{(aq)} + H_{2(g)}$ ☐

[1]

c) In the balanced symbol equation, RuOH has the state symbol (aq). What does this state symbol mean?

....
[1]

d) Rubidium is much more reactive than lithium, sodium or potassium with water. Suggest why it is not safe to carry out the reaction of rubidium with water in a school laboratory.

....
[1]
[Total 4 marks]

Chapter C2 — Chemical Patterns

5 The element francium is below caesium in Group 1 of the periodic table. Even though it is very rare, we can still make predictions about francium's properties and reactions.

a) The boiling point of francium is lower than the boiling point of caesium. Explain why.

....

....

....
[3]

b) Like the other alkali metals, francium can react with chlorine to form a metal halide.

   i) Give the formula of the metal halide that would form if francium reacted with chlorine.

   ....
   [1]

   ii) Explain why francium reacts in a similar way to the other alkali metals.

   ....
   [1]
   [Total 5 marks]

6 The Group 1 metals sodium and potassium both react with water. The reaction of potassium with water is faster and more violent than the reaction of sodium with water.

a) Explain why potassium is more reactive than sodium.

....

....

....

....
[3]

b) Describe an experiment that you could do to show that the reaction of potassium with water is faster than the reaction of sodium with water.

....

....

....

....
[3]
[Total 6 marks]

Exam Practice Tip

There are three main reactions of the Group 1 elements that you need to learn about: how they react with moist air, chlorine and cold water. You also need to know the trends in the properties of the elements and the reasons why these trends exist.

Group 7 Elements and Their Reactions

1 Draw **one** line from each set of reactants to their product.

Reactants

bromine + lithium

iodine + potassium

bromine + sodium

Product

lithium iodide

potassium iodide

lithium bromide

sodium bromide

[Total 3 marks]

2 The elements in Group 7 of the periodic table are known as the halogens.

a) Which of the following statements about the halogens is true?
Place a tick (✓) in the box next to the correct answer.

They are non-metals that exist as single atoms. ☐

They are metals that exist as single atoms. ☐

They are non-metals that exist as molecules of two atoms. ☐

They are metals that exist as molecules of two atoms. ☐

[1]

b) Describe the state and appearance of chlorine at room temperature and pressure.

....

[2]
[Total 3 marks]

3 Sophia carries out a reaction between chlorine gas and lithium.

a) During Sophia's reaction, the salt lithium chloride, LiCl, forms.
Write the balanced symbol equation for this reaction.

....

[2]

b) Sophia carries out a second reaction using iodine and sodium.
Give the formula of the salt that would be formed by this reaction.

....

[1]
[Total 3 marks]

Chapter C2 — Chemical Patterns

4 Halogens and halide salts can take part in halogen displacement reactions.

a) Describe what is meant by a displacement reaction.

....
[1]

b) The table shows some experiments between halogens and halide solutions.
Place a tick (✓) in **one** box of each row to show whether or not a reaction will take place.

Halogen Water	Halide Solution	Reaction	No Reaction
chlorine water	potassium bromide		
iodine water	potassium bromide		
bromine water	potassium chloride		
chlorine water	potassium iodide		

[2]

[Total 3 marks]

5 Greg adds a sample of an unknown halogen to three different halide solutions. The table shows the results of each experiment.

Halogen added to:		
Sodium chloride solution	Sodium bromide solution	Sodium iodide solution
no reaction	solution turns orange	solution turns brown

a) Which halogen did Greg add to each of the halide solutions?
Place a tick (✓) in the box next to the correct answer.

bromine ☐   iodine ☐   chlorine ☐   astatine ☐

[1]

b) Explain your answer to part a).

....

....

....
[2]

c) Astatine sits below iodine in Group 7 of the periodic table. Complete the word equation below for the reaction that would take place between chlorine water and sodium astatide solution.

chlorine + sodium astatide → .... + ...

[2]

[Total 5 marks]

Group 0 Elements

1 The Group 0 elements have similar properties. *(Grade 3-4)*

a) Describe the state of the Group 0 elements at room temperature.

....
[1]

b) Which of the following best describes the structure of the Group 0 elements?
Draw a circle around the correct answer.

    molecules containing two atoms   single atoms   ions   metallic

[1]

c) The Group 0 elements are unreactive. Explain why.

....
[1]

[Total 3 marks]

2 There are trends in the properties of the Group 0 elements. *(Grade 4-5)*

a) Complete the table by predicting the boiling point of radon (Rn).

Element	Boiling Point / °C
Ar	−186
Kr	−152
Xe	−108
Rn	....

[1]

b) Explain the trend in boiling points as you go down Group 0.

....

....

....
[3]

[Total 4 marks]

Exam Practice Tip

You need to know why elements in Groups 1 and 7 are reactive and know what they react with. You also need to know why Group 0 elements don't react. Remember it's all about the number of electrons in the outer shell of the elements.

Ions

1 Ions are charged particles.

a) Which of the following statements about ions is correct?
Place a tick (✓) in the box next to the correct answer.

Ions are formed when charges gain or lose electrons. ☐

Ions are formed when neutrons gain or lose electrons. ☐

Ions are formed when atoms gain or lose electrons. ☐

Ions are formed when protons gain or lose electrons. ☐

[1]

b) Compare the relative numbers of protons and electrons that are present in a **negative ion**.

....

....

[1]

[Total 2 marks]

2 Ions are formed from atoms of elements.

a) Chlorine has an atomic number of 17 and forms ions with a single negative charge.
Calculate the number of electrons in a Cl⁻ ion.

....

[1]

b) Magnesium has an atomic number of 12 and forms ions with a 2+ charge.
Calculate the number of electrons in an Mg^{2+} ion.

....

[1]

c) Use words from the box to complete the following sentences about how ions are formed.

free	negative	share	lose
outer shell	positive	gain	

Elements in the same group have the same number of .... electrons.

Group 1 elements .... electrons to form .... ions.

Group 7 elements .... electrons to form .... ions.

[5]

[Total 7 marks]

Chapter C2 — Chemical Patterns

Ionic Bonding

1 Ionic bonds form when ions are attracted to each other. *Grade 3-4*

a) When metal and non-metal atoms react together, they form positive and negative ions.
State the type of element, metal or non-metal, that forms each type of ion.

Positive ion: ....

Negative ion: ....
[1]

b) Ionic compounds form from metals and non-metals.
In which of the following compounds are the particles held together by ionic bonds?
Place ticks (✓) in the boxes next to the **two** compounds that you think are ionic.

calcium chloride ☐   carbon dioxide ☐   phosphorus trichloride ☐

potassium oxide ☐   nitrogen monoxide ☐
[2]
[Total 3 marks]

2 The dot and cross diagram below shows lithium fluoride being formed from its elements. *Grade 4-5*

a) Complete the diagram by:
- adding an **arrow** to show the transfer of electron(s)
- adding the charges of the ions
- completing the outer shell electronic structure of the chloride ion

[3]

b) Name the force that holds the ions together in an ionic bond.

....

....
[1]

c) State how you can tell from a dot and cross diagram that
the particles in a compound are held together by ionic bonds.

....

....
[1]
[Total 5 marks]

Exam Practice Tip
Understanding how ionic compounds are formed can be a bit tricky. Remember that no electrons disappear, they just move. The best way to get your head round it is to practise drawing dot and cross diagrams for lots of ionic compounds.

Chapter C2 — Chemical Patterns

Ionic Compounds

Warm-Up

Circle the correct words or phrases in the passage below.

Ionic compounds have <u>giant lattice</u>/<u>simple molecular</u> structures. Solid ionic compounds <u>do</u>/<u>don't</u> conduct electricity, because the ions <u>can</u>/<u>can't</u> move.

Ionic compounds have <u>high</u>/<u>low</u> melting points and boiling points.

1 Potassium bromide is an ionic compound made of potassium ions and bromide ions.

a) Complete the diagram below to show the position of the ions in potassium bromide. Write a symbol in each circle to show whether it is a potassium ion (K^+) or a bromide ion (Br^-).

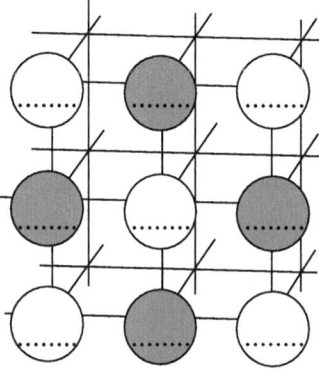

[1]

b) Give **one** disadvantage of using the type of diagram above to show the structure of an ionic compound.

....

....

[1]

[Total 2 marks]

2 Potassium can react with oxygen to form the ionic compound potassium oxide.

a) What is the overall charge on the compound potassium oxide?

....

[1]

b) Potassium oxide is made up of K^+ and O^{2-} ions. What is the chemical formula of potassium oxide?

....

[1]

[Total 2 marks]

Chapter C2 — Chemical Patterns

Chapter C3 — Chemicals of the Natural Environment

Metallic Bonding

Warm-Up

Circle the properties shown below that are properties of metals.

Thermal insulator   Easy to shape   Hard to shape   Thermal conductor

1 The bonding in metals is known as metallic bonding. *(Grade 1-3)*

Place a tick (✓) in the box next to the statement that is **incorrect**.

In a metal, atoms are held together in a giant structure. ☐

Metallic bonds are caused by electrostatic attractions. ☐

Metals can conduct electricity. ☐

Most metals have low boiling points. ☐

[Total 1 mark]

2 The diagram on the right shows the structure of a pure metal. *(Grade 4-5)*

a) Name the particles that are labelled with an **X** in the diagram.

....

[1]

b) Metal atoms form ions that are positively charged. Explain how they are held together in the structure seen in the diagram.

....

....

[2]

c) Most metals have high melting points. Explain why.

....

....

[2]

d) Metal atoms are held together in layers. These layers can slide over each other. Give **two** examples of properties of metals that result from their layered structure.

1. ....

2. ....

[2]

[Total 7 marks]

Reactivity and Reactions of Metals

1 The diagram below shows part of the reactivity series of metals.

Potassium	K
Sodium	Na
Magnesium	Mg
Copper	Cu

Most Reactive ↓ Least Reactive

a) Name **one** metal from the diagram that is more reactive than magnesium.

....
[1]

b) Which metal in the diagram forms positive ions most easily?

....
[1]

c) A student has samples of three metals.
Briefly describe an experiment that he could do to work out an order of reactivity for the metals. Explain how he could use the results to put the metals in order of reactivity.

....

....

....
[2]

[Total 4 marks]

2 A student was investigating the reactions of some metals. She added some calcium (Ca) to a solution of iron sulfate ($FeSO_4$). A reaction took place.

a) Write a word equation for the reaction that took place.

....
[1]

b) What is the name given to this type of reaction?

....
[1]

c) The student then added lead to a solution of iron sulfate. No reaction took place. Explain why.

....
[1]

[Total 3 marks]

Exam Practice Tip

Learning the order of the reactivity series could be helpful when it comes to answering exam questions. If you want to learn it, you could try a mnemonic, like: <u>P</u>lease <u>S</u>on, <u>C</u>atch <u>M</u>e <u>A</u> <u>C</u>ardboard <u>Z</u>ebra — <u>I</u> <u>L</u>ike <u>H</u>ippos <u>C</u>ounting <u>S</u>inks. (That's: Potassium, Sodium, Calcium, Magnesium, Aluminium, Carbon, Zinc, Iron, Lead, Hydrogen, Copper, Silver.)

Chapter C3 — Chemicals of the Natural Environment

More Reactions of Metals

1   Amal performed some experiments to investigate the reactivity of metals.

a) First, Amal placed pieces of four different metals into dilute hydrochloric acid. The diagram below shows what the four experiments looked like after 1 minute.

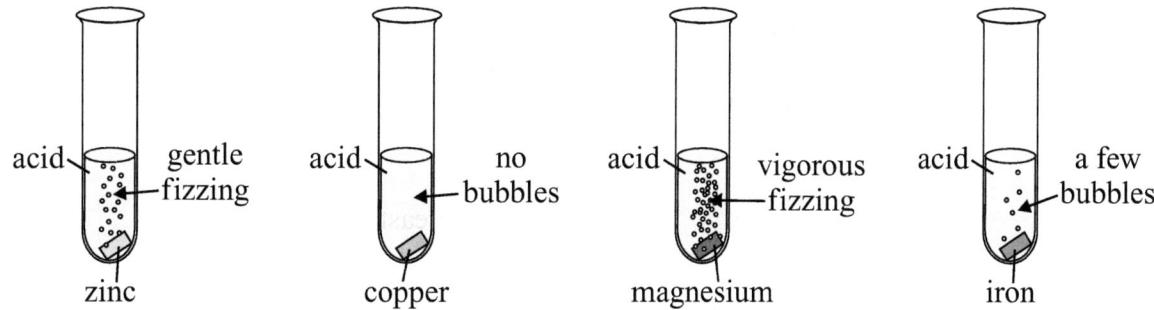

Use the information in the diagram to put these metals in order of reactivity.

Most reactive: ....

....

....

Least reactive: ....

[2]

b) Next, Amal was given samples of three mystery metals, marked **X**, **Y** and **Z**. She put small pieces of each of the metals in water. Her results are shown in the table below.

Metal	Any reaction with water?
X	Reacts vigorously. Hydrogen gas is produced.
Y	Reacts more gently than X. Hydrogen gas is produced.
Z	no reaction

i) Metal **Y** was calcium. Write a word equation for the reaction of calcium with water.

....

[1]

ii) One of the other metals Amal was given was potassium. Suggest whether potassium was metal **X** or metal **Z**. Give a reason for your answer.

....

....

[1]

[Total 4 marks]

Extracting Metals

1 The method used to extract metals from their ores can be determined using the reactivity series. The reactivity series of some elements is shown below.

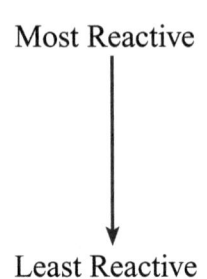

Potassium	K	Most Reactive
Sodium	Na	
Calcium	Ca	
Carbon	C	
Iron	Fe	
Lead	Pb	
Copper	Cu	Least Reactive

a) Tick the correct box in each row to show how the metal is extracted from its ore.

Metal	Extracted using reduction with carbon	Extracted using electrolysis
Calcium		
Copper		
Iron		

[3]

b) Name **one** metal from the reactivity series above which is **not** shown in the table in part a) that could be extracted from its ore using reduction with carbon.

....

[1]

[Total 4 marks]

2 Zinc can be extracted from zinc oxide (ZnO) by reduction with carbon.

a) What does it mean to say that a substance has been 'reduced'?

....

[1]

b) During this process, zinc oxide is heated with carbon. Zinc and carbon dioxide are formed. Write a balanced symbol equation for this reaction.

....

[2]

c) Zinc could also be extracted from its ore using electrolysis. Give **one** disadvantage of using electrolysis to extract metals.

....

[1]

[Total 4 marks]

Electrolysis

Warm-Up

Look at the diagram on the right. Write the labels shown below on the correct lines to identify the parts of an electrochemical cell.

Electrode   Electrolyte
        Power supply

---

1 Electrochemical cells contain electrodes in an electrolyte.

a) What are electrodes?
Place a tick (✓) in the box next to the correct answer.

Solids that conduct electricity. ☐

Solids that react with the electrolyte. ☐

Solids that don't conduct electricity. ☐

Solid ionic compounds. ☐

[1]

b) In electrolysis, the anode is the positive electrode and the cathode is the negative electrode. Describe how the ions move relative to the electrodes in electrolysis.

....

....

[2]

[Total 3 marks]

2 Lead bromide can be electrolysed. The electrolyte is molten lead bromide.

a) What is an electrolyte?

....

[1]

b) Write a word equation for the electrolysis of lead bromide.

....

[1]

c) During this reaction, at which electrode do positive ions gain electrons?

....

[1]

[Total 3 marks]

Chapter C3 — Chemicals of the Natural Environment

3 The diagram below shows the extraction of aluminium using electrolysis. Aluminium oxide is mixed with cryolite. This mixture is then melted and electrolysed to form metallic aluminium and oxygen gas.

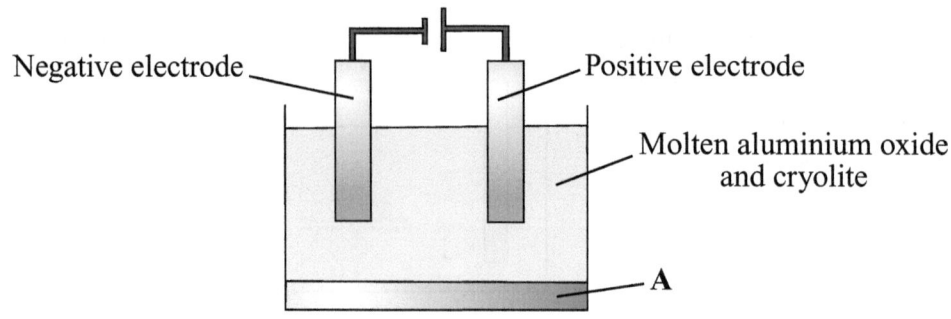

a) Name the liquid labelled **A**.

....
[1]

b) During this process, aluminium oxide (Al_2O_3) is broken down to aluminium metal and oxygen. Write a balanced symbol equation for this reaction.

....
[2]

[Total 3 marks]

4 A student wants to set up an electrochemical cell to carry out electrolysis. He places two inert electrodes into a beaker filled with sodium chloride solution.

a) Describe how the student should prepare the electrodes before placing them in the beaker.

....
[1]

b) Suggest why the electrodes that the student uses need to be **inert**.

....
[1]

c) Which of the following ions is **not** present in sodium chloride solution? Draw a circle around the correct answer.

Cl^- Na^+ OH^- O^{2-}

[1]

d) In this reaction, hydrogen is formed at the cathode rather than sodium. Explain why.

....
[1]

e) State what element is formed at the anode.

....
[1]

[Total 5 marks]

Covalent Bonding

1 Covalent bonds form between two non-metal atoms.

a) What is a covalent bond?

....
[1]

b) Why do non-metal atoms form covalent bonds?

....
[1]

[Total 2 marks]

2 The diagrams below show dot and cross diagrams of some covalent molecules.

a) Draw out the displayed formulas of these molecules using straight lines to represent covalent bonds. The displayed formula of molecule **A** has been done as an example.

Dot and cross diagram   **Displayed formula**

A   (Cl–Cl dot and cross)   Cl — Cl

B   (NH₃ dot and cross)

C   (H₂O dot and cross)

[2]

b) Write out the molecular formula of molecule **B**.

....
[1]

c) Give **one** problem with using dot and cross diagrams to represent covalent molecules.

....
[1]

[Total 4 marks]

Chapter C3 — Chemicals of the Natural Environment

Simple Covalent Substances

1   Ethane (C_2H_6) is a simple covalent substance.

   a) Compare the strength of the bonds that hold the atoms in an ethane
      molecule together with the forces that exist between different molecules.

      ....

      ....
      [2]

   b) Explain why the melting and boiling point of ethane is relatively low.

      ....

      ....
      [1]

   c) Explain why ethane doesn't conduct electricity.

      ....
      [1]

      [Total 4 marks]

2   In each molecule of methane (CH_4), one carbon atom is covalently
    bonded to four hydrogen atoms. Dot and cross diagrams of the
    outer shells of hydrogen and carbon atoms are shown below.

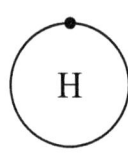   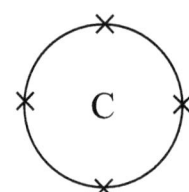

   Draw a dot and cross diagram to show the bonding in **one molecule** of methane.
   You only need to include the outer shell electrons of each atom.

   [Total 2 marks]

Exam Practice Tip

You might be asked about melting and boiling points of simple covalent substances. Remember, when a substance boils (or melts), the intermolecular forces <u>between</u> the molecules break. The covalent bonds <u>within</u> the molecules don't break.

Chapter C3 — Chemicals of the Natural Environment

Empirical Formulas

Warm-Up

Complete the sentences below using words from the box.

| protons | atoms | molecular | empirical |

The .... formula tells you the smallest whole number ratio

of .... in a compound. You can work it out using the

.... formula of the compound.

1 A compound has the molecular formula C_2H_4. What is its empirical formula?
Place a tick (✓) in the box next to the correct answer.

CH_2 ☐ C_4H_8 ☐ C_2H ☐ CH ☐

[Total 1 mark]

2 A compound has the empirical formula C_2H_6N.
Which of the following could be the molecular formula of the compound?
Place a tick (✓) in the box next to the correct answer.

CH_3N ☐ $C_4H_6N_2$ ☐ $C_6H_2N_3$ ☐ $C_4H_{12}N_2$ ☐

[Total 1 mark]

3 Decaborane is a compound with the molecular formula $B_{10}H_{14}$.

What is the empirical formula of decaborane?

empirical formula = ...
[Total 1 mark]

4 Compound Q has the empirical formula CH_2.
The relative formula mass of compound Q is 42.

What is the molecular formula of compound Q?
(relative atomic masses: H = 1, C = 12)

molecular formula = ...
[Total 3 marks]

   Chapter C3 — Chemicals of the Natural Environment

Homologous Series and Alkanes

Warm-Up

Put each of the compounds below into the correct column of the table depending on whether or not they are hydrocarbons.

C_3H_8 C_2H_4

CH_3CH_2Cl

C_2H_6 HCl

Hydrocarbon	Not a hydrocarbon

1 A homologous series is the name given to a family of molecules. The alkanes are a family of hydrocarbon molecules.

a) What is a hydrocarbon?

....
[2]

b) Give the general formula of the alkanes.

....
[1]

c) The **viscosity** of a compound is a measure of how easily it flows. Suggest what effect increasing the length of the carbon chain would have on the viscosity of the alkanes.

....
[1]

[Total 4 marks]

2 A scientist has samples of two hydrocarbons, **A** and **B**. The boiling point of hydrocarbon **A** is 380 °C. The boiling point of hydrocarbon **B** is 235 °C.

a) Which of the two hydrocarbons has a longer carbon chain? Explain your answer.

....

....
[2]

b) Predict which of the two hydrocarbons would be easiest to set on fire. Explain your answer.

....

....
[1]

[Total 3 marks]

Chapter C3 — Chemicals of the Natural Environment

Fractional Distillation of Crude Oil

1 The diagram on the right shows a fractionating column. They are used in the fractional distillation of crude oil.

a) Where does crude oil enter the fractionating column?
Place a tick (✓) in the box next to the correct answer.

A ☐   B ☐   C ☐   D ☐   *[1]*

b) Which is the hottest part of the fractionating column?
Place a tick (✓) in the box next to the correct answer.

A ☐   B ☐   C ☐   D ☐   *[1]*

c) Where do the shortest hydrocarbons leave the fractionating column?
Place a tick (✓) in the box next to the correct answer.

A ☐   B ☐   C ☐   D ☐

[1]

[Total 3 marks]

2 In a fractionating column, the fraction of crude oil are separated on the basis of their boiling points.

a) Explain what is meant by a 'fraction' of crude oil.

....

....
[1]

b) i) Explain why long hydrocarbon molecules have higher boiling points than shorter ones.

....

....

....
[2]

ii) Hydrocarbon **X** is part of a fraction that leaves the fractionating column near the bottom. What does this tell you about the length of hydrocarbon **X**? Explain your answer.

....

....

....

....
[4]

[Total 7 marks]

Uses of Crude Oil

1 An oil refinery processes some fractions of crude oil by cracking them.

a) What happens to large hydrocarbon molecules during cracking?

....
[1]

b) What is the formula of the missing product in the following cracking equation?
Place a tick (✓) in the box next to the correct answer.

$$C_{12}H_{26} \rightarrow C_2H_4 + \ldots\ldots\ldots$$

$C_{10}H_{20}$ ☐ $C_{12}H_{24}$ ☐ $C_{10}H_{22}$ ☐ C_8H_{24} ☐

[1]

c) Name **two** types of hydrocarbons that are produced as a result of cracking.

1. ....

2. ....
[2]

d) Explain why some long-chain hydrocarbons are cracked.

....
[1]

[Total 5 marks]

2 Crude oil has many uses in modern life.

a) Crude oil is a finite resource. What is meant by the term 'finite resource'?

....
[1]

b) Give **two** uses of hydrocarbons obtained from crude oil.

1. ....

2. ....
[2]

c) Suggest **one** thing that could be done to reduce the amount of crude oil we use.

....
[1]

[Total 4 marks]

Exam Practice Tip

In the exam you might get asked to write an equation for a cracking process. The number of C and H atoms in the alkane that's being cracked have to be the same as in the products that are formed. Make sure to count up the number of atoms on both sides of the equation to double check that they're the same.

Chapter C3 — Chemicals of the Natural Environment

Chapter C4 — Material Choices

Polymers

1 All of the plastics we use in everyday life are polymers.

a) What is a polymer?

....
[1]

b) Compare the size of polymers and simple covalent molecules.

....
[1]

c) Describe how the strength of the forces between polymer molecules is affected by the size of the molecules.

....

....
[1]

[Total 3 marks]

2 Different polymers have different properties.

a) Describe how the amount of space between chains in a polymer affects its stiffness.

....

....
[1]

b) Brittany is investigating what happens when she heats two polymers, **A** and **B**.

  i) Brittany says that the melting point of each polymer is determined by the strength of the bonds between the atoms in the polymer chains. Explain why Brittany is wrong.

....

....
[1]

  ii) Brittany's results are shown in the table below.

	Heat to 50 °C	Heat to 100 °C	Heat to 150 °C
Polymer A	Nothing happens.	Melts.	Melts.
Polymer B	Nothing happens.	Nothing happens.	Nothing happens.

Suggest which polymer, **A** or **B**, has crosslinks between its chains. Explain your answer.

....

....
[1]

[Total 3 marks]

Giant Covalent Structures

1 Some molecules have giant covalent structures. *Grade 3-4*

a) What is meant by the term 'giant covalent structure'?

....
[1]

b) To melt a giant covalent compound, the covalent bonds between atoms must be broken.
Explain why this causes giant covalent compounds to have very high melting points.

....

....
[2]

[Total 3 marks]

2 Carbon can form different structures. *Grade 4-5*

a) What is the maximum number of covalent bonds that a carbon atom can form?

....
[1]

b) Diamond is used to make drill tips because it is very hard.
Explain why the structure of diamond makes it so hard.

....

....
[2]

c) Graphite is often used to make electrodes.
Explain why the structure of graphite makes it suitable for use as an electrode.

....

....
[2]

d) Graphene is a single sheet of graphite.
Describe how the carbon atoms are arranged in graphene.

....

....
[2]

[Total 7 marks]

Exam Practice Tip
You've got to know all about the properties of giant covalent structures, like diamond and graphite. But remember, it's not enough just to know what their properties are — you've got to be able to <u>explain why</u> they have those properties too.

Bulk Properties of Materials

Warm-Up

Match the property with the arrangement of particles that causes it.

Easily reshaped	Bonds break when particles move
Strong	Particles move without bonds breaking
Brittle	Particles held firmly in place

1 The bulk properties of materials depend on interactions between particles. *(Grade 1-3)*

a) Place a tick (✓) in the box next to the statement about hardness which is **true**.

Hard materials will not break if they are hit by a sudden force. ☐

Hard materials are difficult to cut. ☐

The hardness of a material is a measure of how difficult it is to shape. ☐

Generally, a material with weak interactions between particles will be hard. ☐

[1]

b) Define the term 'melting point'.

....

[1]

c) What is the term use to describe materials that bend easily without breaking?

....

[1]

[Total 3 marks]

2 The properties of materials are related to their bonding and structure. *(Grade 4-5)*

a) Sodium chloride (NaCl) is an ionic compound. Explain why sodium chloride does **not** conduct electricity when it is a solid.

....

....

[2]

b) Compare the melting points of sodium chloride and methane (a simple molecular compound). Explain your answer in terms of the forces between the particles.

....

....

....

[3]

[Total 5 marks]

Chapter C4 — Material Choices

Types of Materials and Their Uses

1 Different materials are suited to different uses.

a) Place a tick (✓) in the box next to the statement that is **incorrect**.

Ceramics are insulators of heat. ☐

Ceramic materials are good electrical conductors. ☐

Ceramics are usually brittle. ☐

Materials made from ceramics generally last longer than those made from polymers. ☐

[1]

b) Give **two** examples of types of ceramics.

1. ....

2. ....

[2]

c) Ceramics can be used as building materials.
State **one** property of ceramics that makes them suitable for this purpose.

....

[1]

[Total 4 marks]

2 Materials can be categorised into several different types.

a) Match each of the materials with the group of materials it belongs to.

Polystyrene	Metal
Zinc	Polymer
Carbon fibre	Composite

[2]

b) Describe what composite materials are.

....

[1]

c) What determines the properties of a composite?

....

[1]

[Total 4 marks]

Chapter C4 — Material Choices

3 Chris has a garden shed with a roof made from steel sheets, which contain iron. After a few months he notices that the roof is starting to rust.

a) When iron rusts, the iron atoms gain oxygen. What is this process called?

....
[1]

b) Chris wants to replace the roof with a new material that won't corrode. The table below shows some information about two different materials Chris could use.

Material	Strength	Cost	Flexibility
Polyvinyl chloride (PVC)	Medium	Low	High
Carbon fibre	High	High	Low

i) Give **one** advantage of using each type of material for roofing.

Polyvinyl chloride: ....

Carbon fibre: ....
[2]

ii) Give **one** disadvantage of using carbon fibre composite for roofing.

....
[1]
[Total 4 marks]

4 A sports company is choosing a material for making a hockey stick. The material needs to be light and strong. The table below shows data about some materials they could use.

Material	Density (g/cm³)	Relative strength
Carbon fibre	1.5	10
Aluminium alloy	2.5	7
Steel	7.8	8

a) Name **one** material from the table that would **not** be suitable for the stick. Explain your answer.

....

....
[2]

b) Name **one** extra piece of information about the materials that the company might want to know before they make a decision about what material to use.

....
[1]
[Total 3 marks]

Exam Practice Tip

You may be given a list of materials and be asked to decide which one is the most suitable for making something. Physical properties are important, but don't forget to look at cost — e.g. carbon fibre is strong but also very expensive.

Chapter C4 — Material Choices

Reuse and Recycling

Warm-Up

Place a tick (✓) in the correct box next to each of the statements.

Statement	True	False
Recycling materials reduces the amount of waste sent to landfill.		
Recycling is always cheaper than making new materials from scratch.		
Recycling materials often uses less energy than making new ones.		
Recycling materials saves some of the finite resources in the Earth.		

1   Rachel is sorting some rubbish around her house.

Rachel has three pieces of rubbish made from three different materials, **A**, **B** and **C**.
Some data about the materials is in the table below.

Material	Availability of resource	Energy to recycle	Energy to extract
A	Abundant	High	Low
B	Limited	Low	High
C	Limited	Medium	Medium

a) Suggest which material, **A**, **B** or **C**, would be cheapest to recycle. Explain your answer.

....

....
[2]

b) Give **two** reasons why it may not be viable to recycle material **A**.

1. ....

2. ....
[2]

c) The energy used to extract materials comes from burning fossil fuels.
Suggest **one** reason why high energy extraction processes may be a problem.

....

....
[1]

d) Which material, **B** or **C**, do you think would be most suitable to recycle? Explain your answer.

....

....
[1]

[Total 6 marks]

Chapter C4 — Material Choices

Life Cycle Assessments

1 What is the purpose of a life cycle assessment?
Place a tick (✓) in the box next to the statement that is **correct**.

It looks at how many different chemicals are used during the life cycle of a product. ☐

It looks at the total amount of greenhouse gases produced during the life of a product. ☐

It looks at every stage of a product's life to assess the impact on the environment. ☐

It looks at the total economic impact of each stage of a product's life. ☐

[Total 1 mark]

2 A mobile phone company is carrying out a life cycle assessment for a new phone.

a) Describe **one** environmental problem that may be related to using a metal as a raw material.

....
[1]

b) Suggest **one** possible environmental impact of disposing of the phone when it stops working.

....

....
[1]
[Total 2 marks]

3 A shop is deciding whether to stock plastic bags or paper bags.
To help them decide, they carry out a life cycle assessment for each type of bag. Some information about each bag is shown in the table.

	Plastic bag	Paper bag
Raw materials	Crude oil	Wood
Manufacture	A little waste produced.	Lots of waste produced.
Using the product	Can be reused several times.	Usually only used once.
Disposal	Recyclable. Not biodegradable.	Recyclable and biodegradable.

a) Using the information in the table, give **two** advantages of plastic bags over paper bags.

1. ....

2. ....
[2]

b) Give **two** other pieces of information that are not given in the table, that would help the shop to decide which bag would have the least impact on the environment.

1. ....

2. ....
[2]
[Total 4 marks]

Chapter C4 — Material Choices

Nanoparticles and Their Uses

1 Nanoparticles are tiny particles.

a) The sizes of nanoparticles are often given with the units 'nm'.
What does the unit 'nm' stand for?

....
[1]

b) Compare the sizes of nanoparticles and atoms.

....
[1]

[Total 2 marks]

2 Fullerenes are nanoparticles of carbon.
Use words from the box to complete the following sentences about fullerenes.

| low | strong | high | cubes | balls | weak |

Fullerenes are large molecules shaped like hollow .... or tubes.

Fullerenes have fairly .... melting points for molecular substances.

This is because they have .... intermolecular forces

between their molecules, which need a lot of energy to break.

[Total 3 marks]

3 Nanotechnology is a modern science.

a) Place a tick (✓) in the box next to the statement about nanoparticles which is **true**.

Nanoparticles contain only carbon atoms. ☐

Nanoparticles are 1-100 nm in size. ☐

All nanoparticles are the same size and shape. ☐

Nanoparticles are smaller than atoms. ☐

[1]

b) Define the term 'nanotechnology'.

....
[1]

c) Explain why nanoparticles make good catalysts.

....
[1]

[Total 3 marks]

Chapter C4 — Material Choices

4 Cube **A** is a nanoparticle, with sides that are 10 nm long.

a) Calculate the volume of cube **A**.
Use the formula: volume of cube = side length × side length × side length.

Volume = ... nm³
[1]

b) Calculate the area of one face of cube **A**.
Use the formula: area of square = side length × side length.

Surface area = ... nm²
[1]

c) Given that cubes have six faces, calculate the total surface area of cube **A**.

Surface area = ... nm²
[1]

d) Use your answers to parts a) and c) to find the surface area to volume ratio of cube **A** in its simplest form. Place a tick (✓) in the box next to the answer that is **correct**.

6:10 ☐   5:3 ☐   3:5 ☐   6:1 ☐

[1]
[Total 4 marks]

5* Research has been done into the use of fullerenes in medicines.

Describe the advantages and disadvantages of using fullerenes in medicines. Include ideas about:
- How fullerenes could be used in medicine.
- The risks of using fullerenes in medicine.
- The difficulties in predicting the long term risks of using fullerenes in medicines.

....

....

....

....

....

....

....

....

....

....

[Total 6 marks]

Chapter C5 — Chemical Analysis

Purity and Mixtures

Warm-Up

Tick the boxes to show whether each of the following substances is chemically pure or impure.

	pure	impure
milk	☐	☐
diamond	☐	☐
sea water	☐	☐
carbon dioxide gas	☐	☐

1 Chemists sometimes need samples of pure substances. *Grade 3-4*

a) Give the definition of a pure substance in chemistry.

....

....
[1]

b) Chemists can mix exact amounts of different pure substances to make products such as medicines and paints. What are these types of mixtures called?

....
[1]
[Total 2 marks]

2 A scientist is investigating the purity of different substances by measuring their melting points. *Grade 4-5*

a) The scientist measures the melting points of two samples of copper. Sample **A** had a melting point of 1085 °C and sample **B** melted over the range 900 – 940 °C. Suggest which of the two samples was **pure**. Explain your answer.

....

....
[1]

b) The melting point of pure ice is 0 °C. The scientist takes a sample of frozen salt water and measures the temperature at which it melts. Give **one** way that the addition of salt will affect the melting point of the ice.

....
[1]
[Total 2 marks]

Chromatography

1 The first three steps of the method for carrying out a paper chromatography experiment are shown below. *Grade 3-4* **PRACTICAL**

1. Draw a pencil line near the bottom of a sheet of filter paper.
2. Add a spot of ink to the line.
3. Pour a small amount of solvent into a beaker.

a) Which of the following steps should be done next?
Place a tick (✓) in the box next to the correct answer.

Place a lid on the beaker. ☐

Place the sheet in the solvent so that the solvent is just below the pencil line. ☐

Put a locating agent on the paper. ☐

Let the solvent seep up the paper until it's almost reached the top. ☐

[1]

b) Why is pencil used to make the line on the filter paper instead of pen?

....

[1]
[Total 2 marks]

2 Raqim is using paper chromatography to separate and identify dyes in an ink. *Grade 3-4*

a) Place a tick (✓) in the box next to the **true** statement describing his paper chromatography experiment.

The dyes move in the mobile phase. ☐

The mobile phase is the filter paper. ☐

The stationary phase moves up the mobile phase. ☐

The least soluble dye spends a longer time in the mobile phase. ☐

[1]

b) The dyes in the ink separate out because they move different distances up the paper.
Explain why the dyes travel different distances.

....

....

[1]
[Total 2 marks]

Exam Practice Tip

In paper chromatography, the paper is the stationary phase. If you find that tricky to remember, try thinking about paper being a type of stationery — like pencils, rulers and erasers. And if something is mobile, it's able to move or be moved — like mobile phones. So the mobile phase is the solvent that moves up the paper carrying the substances with it.

Chapter C5 — Chemical Analysis

Interpreting Chromatograms

1   A scientist used chromatography to analyse the composition of five food colourings. Four of the colourings were unknown (**A – D**). The other was sunrise yellow. The results are shown in the diagram below.

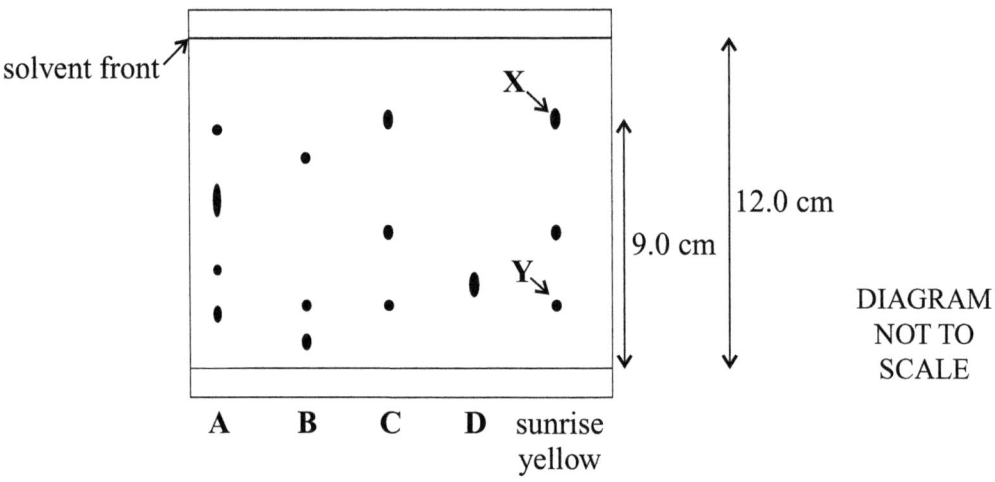

a) Which food colouring, **A**, **B**, **C** or **D**, could be a pure substance?

....

[1]

b) Which of the unknown food colourings, **A**, **B**, **C** or **D**, could be sunrise yellow?

....

[1]

c) Calculate the Rf value for the spot labelled **X** in the diagram.

Use the equation: $Rf = \dfrac{\text{distance moved by solute}}{\text{distance moved by solvent}}$

Rf = ...

[2]

d) The scientist notices that one of spots in food colouring **B** has travelled the same distance as spot **Y** in sunrise yellow. He thinks the same dye might be present in both food colourings. Suggest how he could check this. State what he would see if the dye is in both food colourings.

....

....

....

[2]

[Total 6 marks]

Exam Practice Tip

The Rf value of a substance will always be between 0 and 1. If you're asked to work out an Rf value and find that your result is bigger than 1, check that you've put your numbers in the equation the right way round.

Chapter C5 — Chemical Analysis

Distillation

PRACTICAL

1 A student is using fractional distillation to separate a mixture of liquids. She puts the mixture in a flask and attaches a fractionating column and condenser above the flask.

The table below shows the next five steps in the experiment. Write numbers in the boxes to show the order these steps are carried out in. The first one has been done for you.

Step	Order
The flask is heated slowly.	1
The first liquid is collected.	
The heat is increased until a second substance begins to be collected.	
The substance with the lowest boiling point evaporates and rises up the column.	
The substance with the lowest boiling point condenses and runs down the condenser.	

[Total 4 marks]

2 Propanone is a substance with a boiling point of 56 °C. A sample of propanone contained an impurity with a boiling point of 151 °C. The distillation apparatus shown below was set up to separate propanone from the impurity.

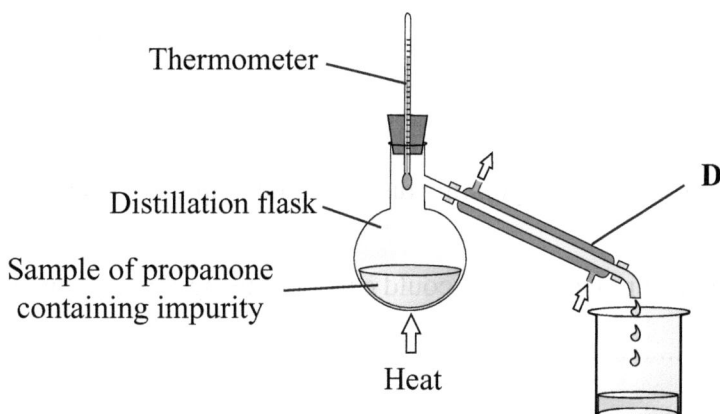

a) Name the piece of apparatus labelled **D**.

   ....
   [1]

b) Explain how propanone will be separated from the impurity using the equipment shown.

   ....
   ....
   ....
   ....
   ....
   [4]

[Total 5 marks]

Chapter C5 — Chemical Analysis

Separating Mixtures

1 Jess carries out a reaction which produces silver chloride, an insoluble salt, and sodium nitrate solution. She wants to separate the silver chloride from the solution.

a) Suggest a separation technique that Jess could use.

....
[1]

b) Place a tick (✓) in the box next to the two pieces of equipment that Jess would need for this separation technique.

Filter paper and funnel ☐

Bunsen burner and filter paper ☐

Distillation flask and condenser ☐

Evaporating dish and funnel ☐

[1]

[Total 2 marks]

2 A mixture is made by dissolving substance **A** (a solid) in water. Some equipment that could be used to separate substance **A** from the solution is shown below.

Beaker   Bunsen burner   Evaporating dish   Filter paper   Funnel   Tripod, gauze and heatproof mat

a) Name the separation technique that you could carry out using this equipment.

....
[1]

b)* Write a method that could be used to separate substance **A** from the water using this equipment.

....

....

....

....

....

....

....
[6]

[Total 7 marks]

Chapter C5 — Chemical Analysis

Relative Mass

1 The relative atomic mass of chlorine is 35.5. The relative atomic mass of hydrogen is 1.0.

a) Calculate the relative formula mass of hydrochloric acid (HCl).

Relative formula mass = ...
[1]

b) Calculate the relative formula mass of chlorine gas (Cl_2).

Relative formula mass = ...
[1]
[Total 2 marks]

2 Match the following formulas with the correct relative formula mass of the substance.

F_2	38.0
C_2H_6	98.1
CaO	30.0
H_2SO_4	56.1

[Total 2 marks]

3 Magnesium oxide is a salt with the molecular formula MgO.
Relative atomic masses (A_r): O = 16.0, Mg = 24.3

Calculate the percentage mass of magnesium in magnesium oxide.
Give your answer to 3 significant figures. Use the equation:

$$\text{Percentage mass of element in a compound} = \frac{A_r \text{ of element} \times \text{number of atoms of element}}{M_r \text{ of compound}} \times 100$$

Percentage mass of magnesium = ... %
[Total 3 marks]

Chapter C5 — Chemical Analysis

Conservation of Mass

1 Iron and sulfur react together to produce iron sulfide. *Grade 1-3*

a) Compare the mass of the reactants with the mass of the products in a reaction.

....
[1]

b) 28 g of iron reacts with 16 g of sulfur. How much iron sulfide is made?
Draw a circle around the correct answer.

    28 g   16 g   44 g   12 g

[1]
[Total 2 marks]

2 A student mixes 3.0 g of silver nitrate solution and 15.0 g of sodium chloride solution together in a flask and seals it with a bung. The following precipitation reaction occurs: *Grade 3-4*

$$AgNO_{3\,(aq)} + NaCl_{(aq)} \rightarrow AgCl_{(s)} + NaNO_{3\,(aq)}$$

Predict the total mass of the contents of the flask after the reaction.

Mass = ... g
[Total 1 mark]

3 When sodium hydroxide reacts with hydrochloric acid, the only products are sodium chloride and water. *Grade 3-4*

a) In an experiment, 80.0 g of sodium hydroxide reacted with 73.0 g of hydrochloric acid. 36.0 g of water was produced. Calculate the mass of sodium chloride produced.

Mass = ... g
[2]

b) Use relative formula masses to show that mass is conserved in the reaction.

$$NaOH + HCl \rightarrow NaCl + H_2O$$

Relative formula masses: NaOH = 40.0, HCl = 36.5, NaCl = 58.5, H_2O = 18.0.

....

....
[3]
[Total 5 marks]

Chapter C5 — Chemical Analysis

4 A student burned 12 g of magnesium in oxygen to produce magnesium oxide.

a) Which of the following is the correctly balanced equation for the reaction between magnesium and oxygen? Place a tick (✓) in the box next to the correct answer.

Mg + O → MgO ☐   2Mg + O$_2$ → 2MgO ☐

Mg + O$_2$ → 2MgO ☐   Mg + O$_2$ → MgO ☐

[1]

b) The student measured the mass of magnesium oxide produced. The mass was 20 g. Calculate the mass of oxygen that reacted with the magnesium.

Mass of oxygen = ... g
[1]
[Total 2 marks]

5 Nathaniel heated some copper carbonate powder. When heated, copper carbonate breaks down to produce copper oxide and carbon dioxide.

Nathaniel measured the mass of the reaction container at the start and at the end of the reaction. The set-up of his experiment and the display of the mass balance are shown below.

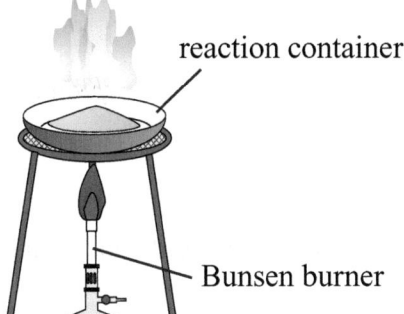

mass at the start of the reaction

mass at the end of the reaction

a) Calculate the change in mass of the reaction container during the reaction.

Change in mass = ... g
[1]

b) Nathaniel thinks that the measurements must be wrong, because no mass is lost or gained in a chemical reaction. Is Nathaniel correct? Explain your answer.

....

....

....

....
[3]
[Total 4 marks]

Acids, Alkalis and Standard Solutions

Warm-Up

The word equations for some neutralisation reactions are shown below.
Complete each word equation by choosing one of the salts from the box.

| calcium chloride | potassium chloride | calcium nitrate |
| calcium sulfate | sodium nitrate | sodium sulfate |

1) hydrochloric acid + calcium hydroxide → .... + water
2) sulfuric acid + sodium hydroxide → .... + water
3) nitric acid + calcium hydroxide → .... + water

---

1 How would you make a standard solution of sodium carbonate?
Place a tick (✓) in the box next to the correct answer.

Carry out simple distillation of a solution of sodium carbonate. ☐

React the correct mass of sodium carbonate with the correct volume of hydrochloric acid. ☐

Dissolve the correct mass of sodium carbonate in the correct volume of deionised water. ☐

Heat a sample of solid sodium carbonate. ☐

[Total 1 mark]

2 Acids and alkalis react together in neutralisation reactions.

a) i) Write the general word equation for a neutralisation reaction between an acid and an alkali.

....
[1]

ii) Write a balanced symbol equation for the neutralisation reaction
between sulfuric acid (H_2SO_4) and potassium hydroxide (KOH).

....
[2]

b) Write an equation that shows how hydrogen ions (H^+) and
hydroxide ions (OH^-) react together during a neutralisation reaction.

.... + ... → ....

[1]
[Total 4 marks]

Exam Practice Tip

Working out the name of a salt made in a neutralisation reaction isn't too tricky. The first part of the name comes from the first part of the alkali — it will be a metal like sodium or calcium. The second part comes from the acid used — nitrates are made from nitric acid, sulfates are made from sulfuric acid and chlorides are made from hydrochloric acid.

Chapter C5 — Chemical Analysis

Titrations

Warm-Up

The diagrams below show a titration experiment being set up.
Label the diagrams using the labels on the right. One label has been done for you.

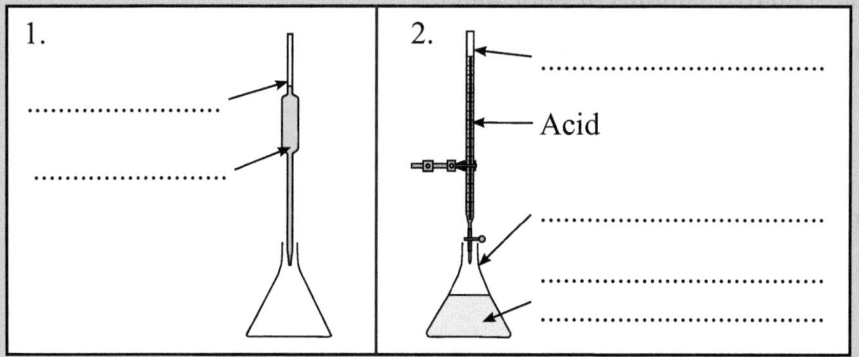

1. Yoshi is carrying out a titration.

   a) Identify which of the following statements is **false**. Place a tick (✓) in one box only.

   Universal indicator is the most suitable indicator for use in titrations. ☐

   Titrations can be used to determine the concentration of an unknown acid or alkali. ☐

   Titrations can show you how much acid is needed to neutralise an alkali. ☐

   An indicator is usually used to identify the end-point in a titration. ☐

   [1]

   b) Before doing an accurate titration, Yoshi does a rough titration. Explain why.

   ....

   ....

   ....
   [2]

   c) The steps of the method for Yoshi's accurate titration are shown below. Step 4 is missing.

   > 1. Use a pipette and a pipette filler to add a set volume of alkali to a conical flask and add a few drops of indicator.
   > 2. Use a funnel to fill a burette with a standard solution of an acid.
   > 3. Record the initial volume of the acid in the burette.
   > 4.
   > 5. Record the volume of acid required to just make the indicator change colour.

   Describe step 4 of the titration method.

   ....

   ....
   [2]

   [Total 5 marks]

Evaluating Titration Data

1. A class is using titration to measure the concentration of hydroxide ions in a swimming pool. They need to collect some pool water to take back to the classroom to test.

   Place a tick (✓) in the box next to the best way for the students to collect representative samples of pool water.

   Take one sample from one corner of the swimming pool. ☐

   Take several samples from one corner of the pool. ☐

   Take several samples from random points throughout the pool. ☐

   Take one sample from each end of the pool. ☐

   [Total 1 mark]

2. Carrie is using titration to find the volume of hydrochloric acid needed to neutralise a sample of sodium hydroxide. First she does a rough titration, then four accurate titrations. The results of her accurate titrations are shown in the table below.

	Titration repeat number			
	1	2	3	4
Initial burette reading (cm³)	5.00	5.00	5.00	5.00
Final burette reading (cm³)	17.30		17.25	17.35
Volume of hydrochloric acid used (cm³)	12.30	12.55	12.25	12.35

   a) Give the final burette reading for titration repeat number **2**.

   .... cm³
   [1]

   b) Carrie decides to work out the mean volume of acid used from titration repeat numbers **1**, **3** and **4**. Calculate the mean volume of hydrochloric acid used in these three titrations.

   .... cm³
   [1]

   c) How does finding a mean make the result more accurate?

   ....
   [1]

   d) Brody says that Carrie should have calculated the mean from all four titrations. Why is Brody wrong?

   ....
   [1]

   [Total 4 marks]

Chapter C6 — Making Useful Chemicals

Acids, Alkalis and pH

Warm-Up

Fill in the gaps in the following statements.

acids   alkalis   neutral

Substances with a pH of less than 7 are ....

Substances with a pH of 7 are ....

---

1 Alice uses Universal Indicator to test the pH of some everyday substances. Her results are shown in the table below.

Substance	Apple juice	Bicarbonate of Soda	Water	Soap
pH	4	9	7	10

a) Write the name of **one** substance in the table that is an alkali.

....
[1]

b) Suggest **one** way that Alice could test the pH of other substances without using an indicator.

....
[1]

[Total 2 marks]

2 The pH of a substance tells you whether it's an acid or an alkali.

a) Which ion is always produced by an acid in aqueous solution?
Place a tick (✓) in the box next to the correct answer.

Cl^- ☐ H^+ ☐ OH^- ☐ OH^+ ☐

[1]

b) Annie adds a few drops of universal indicator to a strong acid. Then she adds exactly the right amount of a strong alkali to neutralise the acid and stirs the mixture carefully. Describe what Annie will see during the course of this experiment.

....

....
[2]

c) State the range of the pH scale.

....
[1]

[Total 4 marks]

Reactions of Acids

1 Draw **one** line from each acid to the type of salt it forms when it reacts with a base.

Acid	Salt
Hydrochloric acid	Nitrate
Nitric acid	Sulfate
Sulfuric acid	Chloride

[Total 2 marks]

2 Theresa is investigating the reactions of acids with metal carbonates. She adds some sodium carbonate to a solution of hydrochloric acid.

a) Which of the following substances will not be produced by Theresa's reaction? Place a tick (✓) in the box next to the correct answer.

A salt ☐ Carbon dioxide ☐ Hydrogen ☐ Water ☐

[1]

b) Name the metal-containing product formed during this reaction.

....

[1]

[Total 2 marks]

3 Sulfuric acid reacts with lithium hydroxide to produce lithium sulfate and one other product.

a) Name the product, other than lithium sulfate, that is produced in this reaction.

....

[1]

b) Lithium sulfate is also made when sulfuric acid reacts with lithium. Which of following is the correct balanced symbol equation for this reaction? Place a tick (✓) in the box next to the correct answer.

$Li + H_2SO_4 \rightarrow Li_2SO_4 + H_2O$ ☐

$2Li + H_2SO_4 \rightarrow Li_2SO_4 + H_2$ ☐

$Li_2 + H_2SO_4 \rightarrow Li_2SO_4 + H_2$ ☐

$Li + 2H_2SO_4 \rightarrow Li_2SO_4 + 2H_2$ ☐

[1]

[Total 2 marks]

Making Salts — PRACTICAL

Warm-Up

Circle the substances below that are salts.

sulfuric acid   sodium chloride   hydrochloric acid   water

copper nitrate   carbon dioxide   zinc sulfate

---

1 Ravi wants to make a pure, dry sample of the salt potassium chloride. He has a bottle of dilute potassium hydroxide and a bottle of dilute hydrochloric acid.

a) Anna thinks that Ravi should begin by adding an excess of the acid to the potassium hydroxide. Explain why this is wrong.

....
[1]

b) Ravi starts by working out how much acid he needs to react exactly with the potassium hydroxide. The diagram below shows the equipment he uses.

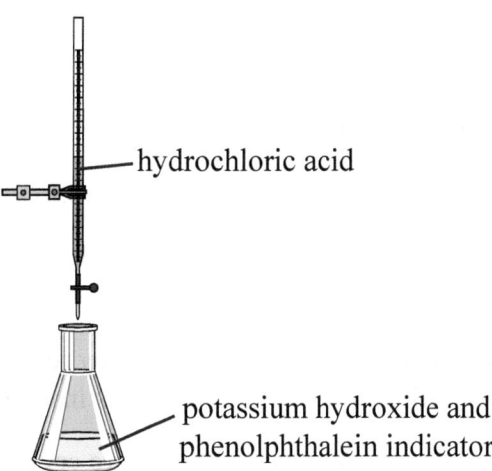

How will Ravi be able to tell when all the alkali has reacted?

....
[1]

c) Dilute hydrochloric acid and dilute potassium hydroxide are both **irritants**. Suggest **one** safety precaution Ravi should take to reduce the risks associated with his experiment.

....
[1]

d) Ravi then makes a solution of potassium chloride by mixing the same volumes of the acid and the alkali. Name the method he should use to produce a solid salt from his solution.

....
[1]

[Total 4 marks]

Chapter C6 — Making Useful Chemicals

2 A student reacts silver nitrate solution with sodium chloride solution to make an insoluble salt containing silver.

a) Name the insoluble salt that forms.

....
[1]

b) Describe how the student could prepare the silver nitrate solution from solid silver nitrate.

....

....
[2]

c) The student used the following method to prepare the insoluble salt:

> 1. Mix the sodium chloride solution with the silver nitrate solution in a beaker and stir.
> 2. Line a filter funnel with filter paper and place it in a conical flask.
>   Pour the contents of the beaker into the filter paper.
> 3. Rinse the beaker with deionised water and tip this into the filter paper.
> 4. Rinse the contents of the filter paper with deionised water.

i) Describe what the student would see during step 1.

....
[1]

ii) What is the purpose of step 3?

....
[1]

[Total 5 marks]

3* Zinc chloride is a soluble salt. It can be made by reacting dilute hydrochloric acid with zinc hydroxide, which is insoluble in water.

Write a method that you could use to make pure crystals of zinc chloride using this reaction.
- Describe how you would make the salt from the reactants.
- Describe how you would purify the salt from the reaction mixture.

....

....

....

....

....

....

....

[Total 6 marks]

Chapter C6 — Making Useful Chemicals

Rates of Reactions

1 You can change the rate of a reaction by changing the reaction conditions.

a) Use words from the box to complete the following sentences about rates of reaction.

| higher | explosive | fast | lower | hot |

The rate of reaction is how .... a reaction is.

Particles have to collide in order to react. The more frequent the collisions are,

the .... the rate of reaction.

[2]

b) Which of the following things would **decrease** the rate of a reaction between a solid and a solution? Draw a circle around the correct answer.

using smaller pieces of solid   using a less concentrated solution   increasing the temperature   adding a catalyst

[1]

[Total 3 marks]

2 Jacob heats 25 cm³ of dilute sulfuric acid to a temperature of 25 °C. He adds 5 g of magnesium ribbon to the acid. He puts the flask containing the reaction mixture on a mass balance and records how fasts the mass of the reaction mixture falls.

a) Jacob repeats his experiment, but this time he heats the acid to 35 °C. How would you expect the rate of this reaction to compare to the rate of reaction at 25 °C?

....

[1]

b) Explain your answer to part a). In your answer you should discuss how changing the temperature will affect the collisions between the reacting particles.

....

....

....

....

....

[4]

[Total 5 marks]

Exam Practice Tip

In the exam you could get asked about any of the factors that affect the rate of reactions, so it's really important that you know them all. You've also got to know why changing each of these factors has an effect on the rate of reaction.

Reaction Rates and Catalysts

1 Which of the following statements about catalysts is **not** true? Place a tick (✓) in the box next to the correct answer.

Catalysts increase the rate of a reaction and get used up in the process. ☐

Enzymes are proteins that act as catalysts for reactions in living cells. ☐

Catalysts provide an alternative reaction pathway for the reaction. ☐

Catalysts lower the activation energy of a reaction. ☐

[Total 1 mark]

2 A scientist carried out a neutralisation reaction with and without a catalyst. She kept all other variables the same for both experiments.

a) The graph below shows the reaction profiles for both reactions.

i) Which label, **A–D**, shows the level of energy of the reactants?

....
[1]

ii) Which label, **A–D**, shows the activation energy for the reaction carried out without a catalyst?

....
[1]

b) The graph on the right shows the volume of gas formed by each reaction over time.

State which reaction, **1** or **2**, was the one where the scientist added the catalyst. Explain how you can tell.

....
....
....
[1]

[Total 3 marks]

Chapter C6 — Making Useful Chemicals

Measuring Reaction Rates — PRACTICAL

1 Jade carries out a reaction that produces a gas. She measures the time it takes for 50 cm³ of gas to be produced. Under different conditions, the rate of the reaction changes.

Use words from the box to complete the following sentences about the experiment.

> more quickly   more slowly   in the same time

If the rate is higher than the rate of the original reaction,

the gas will be produced ....

If the rate is lower than the rate of the original reaction,

the gas will be produced ....

[Total 2 marks]

2 Rob has two bottles of dilute sulfuric acid labelled **A** and **B**. He does not know the exact concentration of the acid in either bottle. He mixes a 30 cm³ sample of Acid **A** with 5 g of marble chips and measures the volume of gas produced. Then he repeats the experiment using Acid **B**. The table below shows his results.

		Time (s)					
		0	10	20	30	40	50
Volume of gas produced (cm³)	Acid A	3	8	10	12	16	19
	Acid B	9	19	25	29	32	35

a) Suggest a piece of equipment that Rob might have used to measure the volume of gas produced.

....

[1]

b) State which acid, **A** or **B**, reacted fastest with the marble chips. Give a reason for your answer.

....

....

[1]

c) What are the dependent and independent variables for Rob's experiment?

Dependent variable: ....

Independent variable: ....

[2]

[Total 4 marks]

Chapter C6 — Making Useful Chemicals

Finding Reaction Rates from Graphs

1 In a reaction that lasted 125 seconds, the mass of the reaction mixture fell by 4.0 g.

Calculate the mean rate of the reaction.
Use the equation: mean rate of reaction = $\dfrac{\text{amount of product formed}}{\text{time taken}}$

.... g/s
[Total 1 mark]

2 Jermaine carries out a reaction between magnesium and hydrochloric acid. He measures the volume of hydrogen gas produced at regular time intervals. He plotted his results on a graph, shown below.

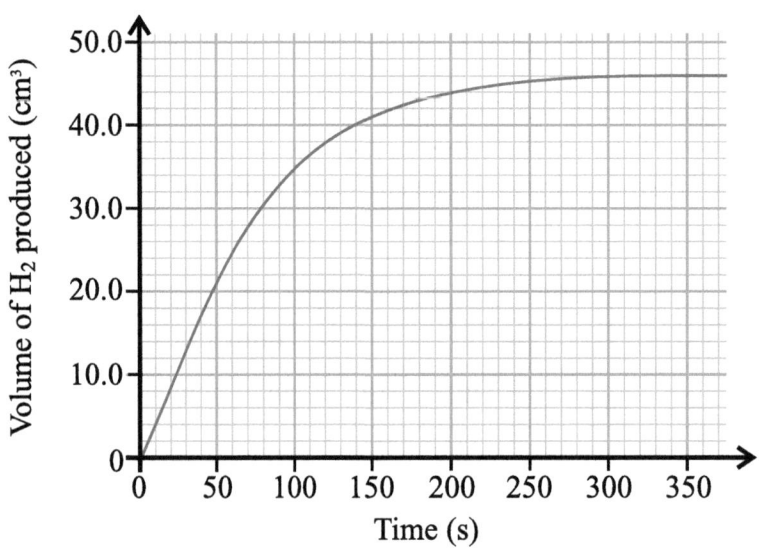

a) Using the graph, find the mean rate for the whole reaction.
Give your answer to 3 significant figures.

mean rate of reaction = $\dfrac{\text{amount of product formed}}{\text{time taken}}$

.... cm^3/s
[2]

b) Using the graph and the formula given in part a), calculate the mean rate of the reaction between 140 seconds and 200 seconds. Give your answer to 2 significant figures.

.... cm^3/s
[4]
[Total 6 marks]

Chapter C6 — Making Useful Chemicals

Using Tangents to Find Reaction Rates

1   The rate of a reaction was investigated by measuring the volume of gas produced at regular intervals. The results are shown in the table.

Time (s)	0	50	100	150	200	250	300
Volume of gas (cm³)	0.0	9.5	14.5	16.0	16.5	16.5	16.5

a) Plot the data in the table on the axes below. Draw a curved line of best fit on the graph.

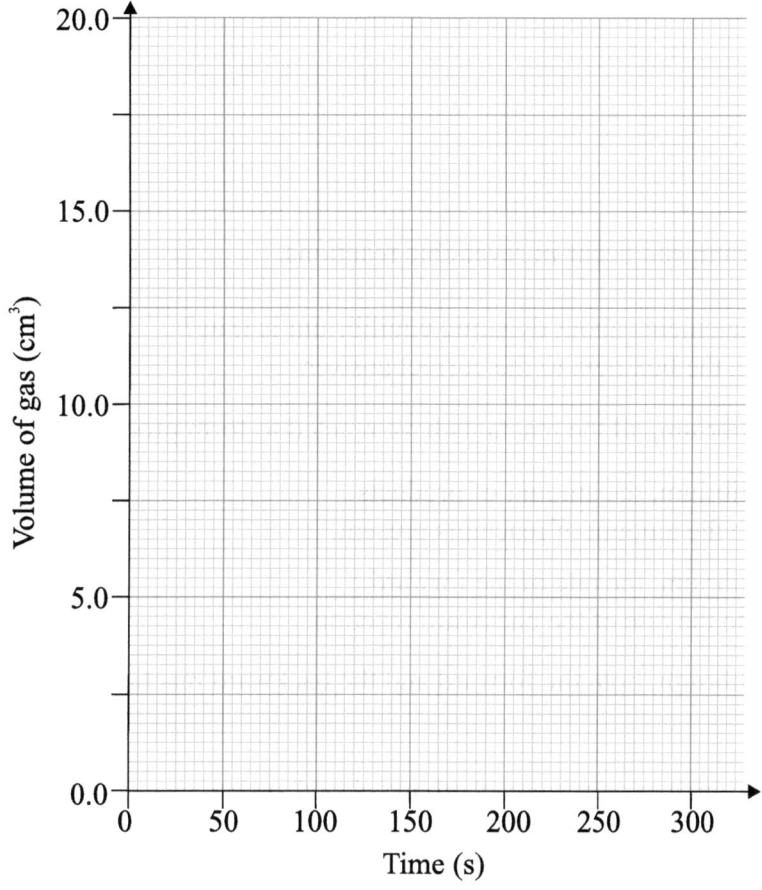

[3]

b) Draw a tangent to the graph at 75 seconds.

[1]

c) Use the tangent that you drew in part b) to find the rate of reaction at 75 s.

.... cm³/s
[3]
[Total 7 marks]

Exam Practice Tip
Plotting graphs is not too tricky, but it can be fiddly, so always make sure to take your time and do it carefully. If you're drawing a tangent, remember that the key thing is to make sure the space between the ruler and the curve is the same on both sides of the point. If you're finding it tricky to draw them, make sure you get plenty of practice before your exams.

Chapter C6 — Making Useful Chemicals

Dynamic Equilibrium

1 The reaction shown below is used to make ammonia. It is a reversible reaction.

a) Put the correct symbol into the reaction equation to show that it is a reversible reaction.

$$N_2 + 3 H_2 \ \text{..................} \ 2 NH_3$$

[1]

b) Explain what the term 'reversible reaction' means.

....

....

[1]

[Total 2 marks]

2 Dynamic equilibrium can occur in reversible reactions.

a) Which of these statements about dynamic equilibrium is **true**?
Place a tick (✓) in the box next to the correct answer.

At dynamic equilibrium, all the reactants have reacted to form products. ☐

At dynamic equilibrium, the amount of products present is equal to the amount of reactants present. ☐

At dynamic equilibrium, the rate of the forward reaction is equal to the rate of the backward reaction. ☐

At dynamic equilibrium, both the forward and the backward reactions stop. ☐

[1]

b) Dynamic equilibrium can only be reached in a closed system.
Explain what is meant by a 'closed system'.

....

....

[1]

c) A reaction is at equilibrium and the equilibrium position lies to the left.
Give **one** factor that you could change in order to change the position of equilibrium.

....

[1]

[Total 3 marks]

Exam Practice Tip

When a reaction's at equilibrium, if there are more products than reactants, then the position of equilibrium is described as lying to the right. If there are more reactants than products, then it's described as lying to the left. But remember, wherever the position of equilibrium is, the forward and backward reactions will still be going at the same rate.

Chapter C6 — Making Useful Chemicals

Chapter P1 — Radiation and Waves

Wave Basics

Warm-Up

Label the waves below with a T or an L to show whether they are transverse waves (**T**) or longitudinal waves (**L**).

sound waves ......   waves on a rope ......   electromagnetic waves ......

1 The diagram below shows a displacement-distance graph of a wave.

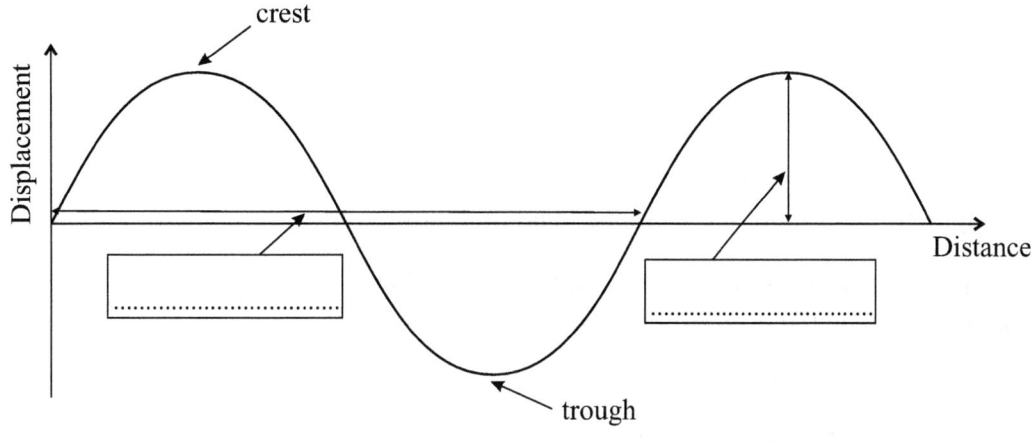

a) Use phrases from the box to complete the labels in the diagram above.

| wavelength | period | rest position | amplitude |

[2]

b) What is the frequency of a wave?

....
[1]

c) Describe a difference between longitudinal waves and transverse waves.

....
....
....
[2]
[Total 5 marks]

2 A child throws a stone into a pond. The stone creates ripples when it hits the water. These ripples spread across the pond.

The child thinks that a leaf floating on the pond will move to the edge of the pond with the ripples. Explain whether or not she is correct.

....
....
....
[Total 2 marks]

Wave Speed

1 A wave has a frequency of 50 Hz and a wavelength of 0.10 m. Calculate the speed of the wave.

Use the equation:

$$\text{wave speed} = \text{frequency} \times \text{wavelength}$$

Wave speed = ... m/s

[Total 2 marks]

2 Clare investigated the speed of sound in air. The equipment she used is shown in the diagram below.

The sound waves detected by each microphone were shown as separate traces on the oscilloscope screen.

a) Her method is described below in steps **A** to **E**.
Steps **A** to **E** are not in the correct order.

A Measure the distance between the microphones. This is the wavelength.
B Stop moving microphone 2 when the traces line up.
C Use the measured distance and the frequency of the signal generator to find the wave speed.
D Begin with both microphones at an equal distance from the speaker.
E Keeping microphone 1 fixed, slowly move microphone 2 away from the speaker, causing trace 2 to move.

In the spaces below, write down the correct order of steps.
The first one has been done for you.

D → .... → .... → .... → ....

[3]

b) The speed of the sound waves was found to be 340 m/s.
The frequency of the signal generator was then changed to 50.0 Hz.
Calculate the wavelength of the sound waves produced.

Wavelength = ... m

[3]

[Total 6 marks]

Chapter P1 — Radiation and Waves

Wave Experiments

PRACTICAL

1 Aria is investigating water waves in a ripple tank. She sets up the equipment shown below.

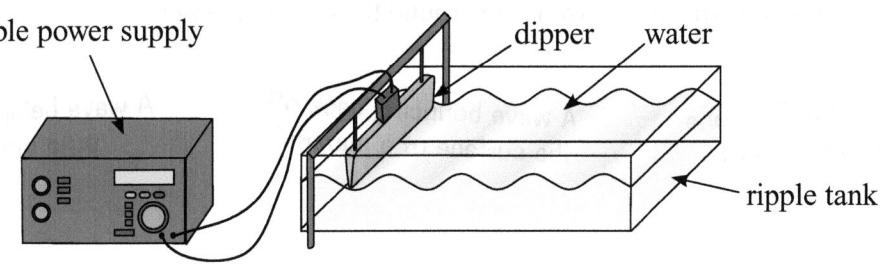

a) Aria wants to measure the frequency of the ripples. She floats a cork in the ripple tank and measures the time it takes for the cork to oscillate 30 times. Aria repeats her experiment five times. She does not adjust the variable power supply between repeats.

State **two** other factors that should remain the same between repeats.

1. ....

2. ....
[2]

b) The table below shows Aria's results. She recorded one of the results incorrectly.

Trial	1	2	3	4	5
Time taken for 30 oscillations (seconds)	36	34	36	34	42

Calculate the average time taken for the cork to oscillate 30 times.

Time for 30 oscillations = ... s
[2]

c) Using your answer to part b), calculate the frequency of the ripples.
Give your answer to **two** significant figures.

Frequency = ... Hz
[3]

d) Aria's friend Cass suggests they could use the ripple tank to measure the speed of the ripples. Describe a method they could use.

....

....

....

....

....

....
[3]
[Total 10 marks]

Reflection

Warm-Up

What does reflection mean? Draw a ring around the correct answer.

A wave passing from one material into another.   A wave bouncing back off the surface of a material.   A wave being absorbed by a material.

1   The diagram below shows a ray of light reflecting off a mirror.

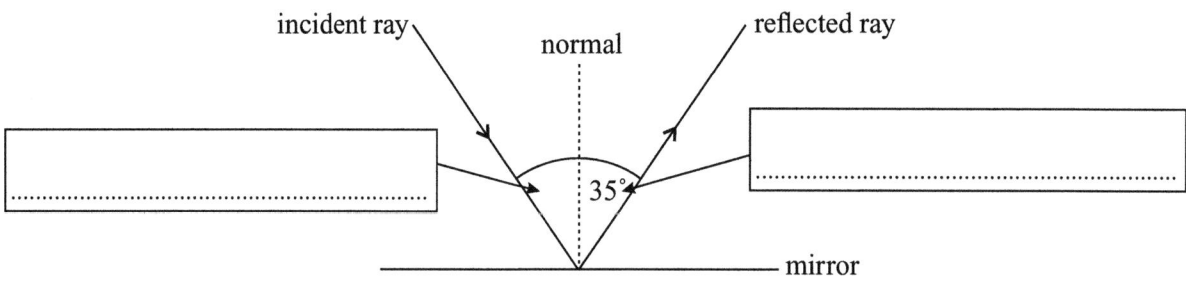

a) Label the angle of incidence and the angle of reflection on the diagram above.

[2]

b) Give the angle between the normal and the incident ray.

Angle = ... °

[1]

[Total 3 marks]

PRACTICAL

2   Ash has a ray box, a mirror and a piece of white paper.
Describe a method that he could use to investigate the relationship between the angle of incidence and the angle of reflection using the equipment.

....

....

....

....

....

....

[Total 4 marks]

Chapter P1 — Radiation and Waves

Refraction

1 A wave crosses the boundary between two materials. This causes it to change direction.

Place a tick (✓) in the boxes next to the **two** correct statements.

The wave has been reflected. ☐

The wave has not travelled along the normal to the boundary between the materials. ☐

The two materials have the same density. ☐

The wave has been refracted. ☐

The wave has been absorbed. ☐

[Total 2 marks]

2 A student wants to model how sound waves behave when they pass from one material into another material.

a) Describe a method that can be used to model the behaviour of sound waves.

....

....

....

....
[2]

b) Give **one** other type of wave that can be modelled in this way.

....
[1]
[Total 3 marks]

3 A ray of light crosses a boundary from air to water. The angle of incidence is 20° and the angle of refraction is 14.9°.

A second ray of light crosses a boundary from water to air. The angle of incidence is 20°. State and explain whether the angle of refraction of this ray will be larger or smaller than 20°.

....

....

....

....
[Total 2 marks]

Chapter P1 — Radiation and Waves

PRACTICAL: Investigating Refraction

1. Ella is investigating the refraction of light through a glass block.
She uses a ray box to shine a ray of light into the block.
She traces the path of the ray entering and leaving the block on a sheet of paper.
She uses this to measure the angles of incidence
and refraction of the light ray entering the block.

Below is an incomplete diagram showing the
path of a ray during the student's investigation.

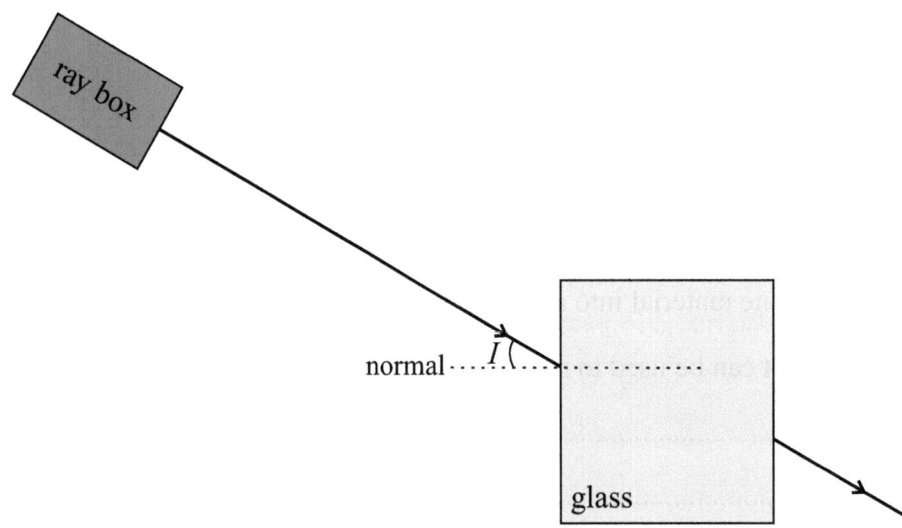

a) Complete the diagram by drawing the light ray as it passes through the glass block.

[1]

b) On the diagram, label the angle of refraction of the light ray as it enters the glass block.

[1]

c) Using the diagram, determine the angle of incidence, *I*,
of the light ray as it enters the glass block.

Angle of incidence = ... °

[1]

d) Ella repeats the experiment for a range of angles of incidence.
Name **two** things the student should do to make her experiment a fair test.

1. ....

2. ....

[2]

[Total 5 marks]

Exam Practice Tip

When drawing rays on a diagram in the exam, make sure you draw them neatly and accurately. Use a sharp pencil and a ruler to help you draw clear, thin, straight lines. And don't forget to add arrows to show which way the rays are going.

The Electromagnetic Spectrum

1 Use phrases from the box below to complete the following sentences.

| cooling | radio waves | X-rays | heating | lose | infrared | gain |

Visible light, ultraviolet radiation and .... can be emitted when electrons in atoms .... energy. Whenever any electromagnetic wave is absorbed, it can cause ....

[Total 3 marks]

2 Ian is studying the Sun. The Sun does not emit gamma rays. It emits all other types of electromagnetic radiation.

a) Name the electromagnetic radiation emitted by the Sun that has the highest energy.

....

[1]

b) Ian makes the following statement.

> **Ian**
> The Sun emits visible light and infrared radiation.
> The infrared radiation is a longitudinal wave.
> It has a longer wavelength than visible light,
> so it takes longer to reach Earth.

Explain why Ian is incorrect.

....

....

....

[2]

c) The Earth's atmosphere is made up of water vapour and many different gases. Suggest why some infrared radiation from the Sun is unable to pass through the atmosphere to the Earth's surface.

....

[1]

[4 marks]

3 Explain how the Earth's atmosphere helps protect animals living on Earth from harmful ultraviolet radiation from the Sun.

....

....

....

[Total 2 marks]

Energy Levels in Atoms

Warm-Up

Use the words in the box to correctly fill in the gaps in the passage.

The .... around a nucleus can sit in different energy levels.

These energy levels are at .... distances from the nucleus.

electrons
protons
different
identical

1 An electron in an atom absorbs electromagnetic radiation. What effect will this have on the energy of the electron and its distance from the nucleus? Place a tick (✓) in each row.

	Decreases	Increases	Stays the same
Energy	☐	☐	☐
Distance from the nucleus	☐	☐	☐

[Total 2 marks]

2 Ultraviolet radiation can harm humans by ionising atoms or molecules in cells.

a) Explain what is meant when an atom is said to have been ionised.

   ....
   [1]

b) Give **two** damaging effects ultraviolet radiation can have on humans.

   1. ....

   2. ....
   [2]

c) Ultraviolet radiation is one type of ionising electromagnetic radiation. Describe how the amount of ionising electromagnetic radiation a person is exposed to affects the type of damage done to the person's body.

   ....

   ....

   ....

   ....
   [2]
   [Total 5 marks]

Uses of EM Radiation

1 Electromagnetic waves can be used in communication.

Which of the following types of electromagnetic radiation is used in optical fibres?
Place a tick (✓) in the box next to the correct answer.

Radio waves ☐

Ultraviolet ☐

Gamma rays ☐

Visible light ☐

[Total 1 mark]

2 Microwave radiation can be used to cook food.

a) Use words from the box below to complete the sentences.

| emits | reflects | increase | absorbs | decrease |

When food is cooked in a microwave oven, water in the food .... microwaves.

This causes the temperature of the food to ....

[2]

b) Give **one** other use of microwave radiation.

....

[1]
[Total 3 marks]

3 Police helicopters use infrared cameras to help them find people in hiding.

a) Which of the following statements about infrared radiation is correct?
Place a tick (✓) in the box next to the correct answer.

The hotter the object, the more infrared radiation it gives out. ☐

The colder the object, the more infrared radiation it gives out. ☐

Hot objects give out no infrared radiation. ☐

All objects give out the same amount of infrared radiation. ☐

[1]

b) Give **one** other device that uses infrared radiation.

....

[1]
[Total 2 marks]

Exam Practice Tip

Make sure you know examples of how each type of EM wave can be used — it could be worth marks in the exam.

Chapter P1 — Radiation and Waves

More Uses of EM Radiation

Warm-Up

For each sentence, circle whether it is true or false.

No electromagnetic waves are dangerous to humans. **True / False**

The risks of using electromagnetic waves need to be considered before using them in new ways. **True / False**

1 A man marks his wallet with a security pen.
   The pen contains ink that cannot be seen in visible light.

   a) Describe how ultraviolet waves can be used to identify the man's wallet if it is stolen.

   ....

   ....
   [1]

   b) Which of the following is another use of ultraviolet light?
      Place a tick (✓) in the box next to the correct answer.

      Cooking food ☐

      Communicating by satellite ☐

      Energy efficient lamps ☐

      Sending TV signals ☐
   [1]
   [Total 2 marks]

2 Electromagnetic waves can be used in hospitals.

   a) Medical tracers that emit gamma rays can be used to detect cancer.
      Give **two** other ways gamma rays can be used in hospitals.

      1. ....

      2. ....
      [2]

   b) Give **one** other type of electromagnetic radiation which can be used to detect health problems.
      Describe how the radiation is used.

      Type of EM radiation: ....

      Use: ....

      ....
      [2]
      [Total 4 marks]

Temperature and Radiation

1 Abdul is studying electromagnetic radiation.

Place a tick (✓) in the box next to the correct statement.

All objects emit electromagnetic radiation. ☐
No objects emit electromagnetic radiation. ☐
Only glowing objects emit electromagnetic radiation. ☐
Objects only emit one type of electromagnetic radiation. ☐

[Total 1 mark]

2 Stars A and B have different temperatures. Star B is much hotter than star A. The graph below shows how the intensity of the radiation emitted by star A varies with wavelength.

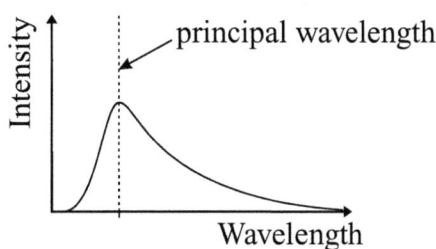

a) Which of the graphs below shows the correct intensity-wavelength distribution for star B? Place a tick (✓) in the box next to the correct graph.
The principal wavelength of star A is marked by the dotted line.

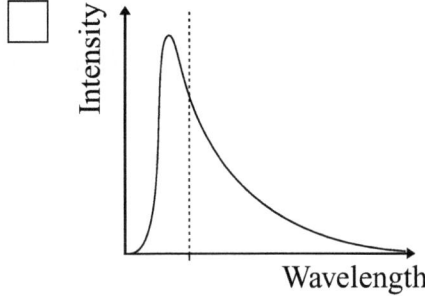
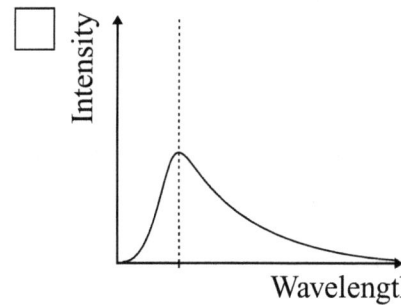

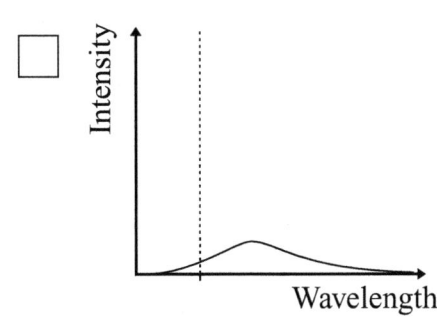
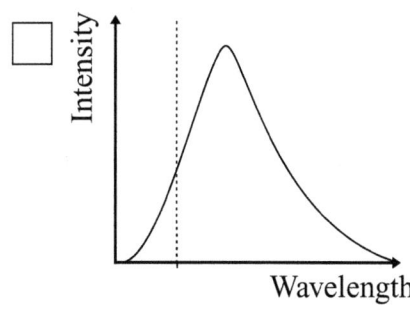

[1]

b) State how the principal frequency of the radiation emitted by a star will change as the star's temperature increases.

....

[1]

[Total 2 marks]

Chapter P1 — Radiation and Waves

Energy Stores and Conservation of Energy

1 Place a tick (✓) in the box next to the statement about energy that is **true**.

Energy can be created and destroyed. ☐

Energy can be created but not destroyed. ☐

Energy can be destroyed but not created. ☐

Energy cannot be created or destroyed. ☐

[Total 1 mark]

2 Draw **one** straight line from each object to the energy store that energy is being transferred **from**.

Object	Energy store
A car slowing down without braking.	chemical energy store
A mug of hot tea cooling down.	thermal energy store
A stretched spring returning to its original shape.	elastic potential energy store
Food being digested.	kinetic energy store

[Total 3 marks]

3 A hot spoon is sealed inside a thermally-insulated flask full of cold water. This is a closed system.

a) Describe a closed system in terms of energy transfers.

....

....

[1]

b) Describe **one** energy transfer that occurs within the closed system.

....

....

[2]

[Total 3 marks]

Exam Practice Tip

In the exams, you might be given a situation and be asked to describe which stores energy is transferred to and from. If you're unsure what energy stores are involved in a transfer, look for clues in the question. For example, if something is lifted above the ground, energy must have been transferred to its gravitational potential energy store.

Energy Transfers

1 An apple falls from a branch of a tree.

Which force does work on the apple and causes it to move towards the ground?
Place a tick (✓) in the box next to the correct answer.

electrostatic force ☐
magnetic force ☐
normal contact force ☐
gravitational force ☐

[Total 1 mark]

2 Use phrases from the box below to complete the passage.

| electrostatic | kinetic | electrically | mechanically | by radiation |

An electric fan is plugged into the mains and switched on.

Energy is transferred .... to the kinetic energy store of the fan's motor.

The energy is then transferred to air particles around the fan ....

The energy is transferred to the air particles' .... energy stores.

[Total 3 marks]

3 Fossil fuels are burnt to release energy. This energy is then transferred electrically to consumers using the national grid.

a) Give **one** advantage of using electricity to transfer energy to consumers.

....
[1]

b) An electric heater is plugged into the mains. It uses the energy from burning fossil fuels to work.

i) Name the energy store energy is released from when fossil fuels are burnt.

....
[1]

ii) The electric heater is turned on. Describe the energy transfers that occur from the mains to the surroundings. You should include how the energy is transferred in your answer.

....

....

....

....
[3]

[Total 5 marks]

Chapter P2 — Sustainable Energy

Efficiency and Power

1 A mobile phone battery has an efficiency of 80%. After being fully charged, the battery transfers 20 000 J of energy usefully before it needs to be charged again.

Calculate the total energy supplied to the battery to fully charge it.
Use the equation:

$$\text{efficiency} = \frac{\text{useful energy transferred}}{\text{total energy transferred}}$$

Total energy supplied = ... J
[Total 3 marks]

2 Riley is using a desk fan to keep her room cool. The desk fan has a power of 35 W.

a) Calculate the energy transferred by the desk fan when it is used for 8.0 hours.
Give your answer in kWh.
Use the equation:

$$\text{energy transferred} = \text{power} \times \text{time}$$

Energy transferred = ... kWh
[3]

b) Riley's brother borrows the fan. While he is using the fan, it transfers 16 800 J of energy. Calculate the time that the fan was on for.

Time = ... s
[3]
[Total 6 marks]

Exam Practice Tip

Remember, efficiency can be given either as a decimal or as a percentage. Make sure you know how to convert between the two forms. If you're substituting it into an equation, you'll usually need the efficiency to be a decimal.

Chapter P2 — Sustainable Energy

Reducing Unwanted Energy Transfers

1 Rich is cycling. Rich does work on the pedals to move the bicycle. Some energy is wasted by the bicycle due to friction between the chain and the gears.

State and explain how Rich could reduce the amount of energy wasted when cycling.

....

....

[Total 2 marks]

2 Gabrielle is trying to minimise the rate at which a house cools.

a) The table shows the types of brick Gabrielle can use to build the walls of the house. Each wall will be made up of a single layer of bricks.
Which type of brick, A, B, C or D, should she use?

	Thermal conductivity	Brick thickness (cm)
A	High	10
B	High	15
C	Low	10
D	Low	15

Your answer = ...
[1]

b) Gabrielle uses her electric drill for 1 minute.
The diagram below shows an incomplete Sankey diagram for the drill during this time.

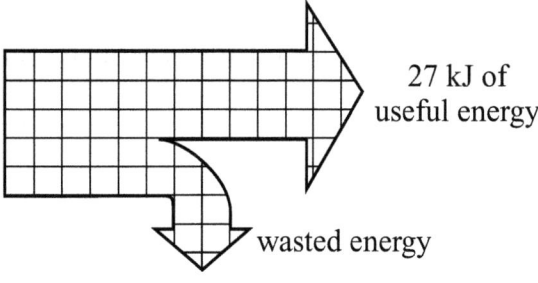

Calculate how much energy is supplied to the drill during 1 minute.

Energy supplied = ... kJ
[3]
[Total 4 marks]

Chapter P2 — Sustainable Energy

Energy Resources

Warm-Up

Circle the non-renewable energy resources below.

coal   wind   uranium   bio-fuels   sunlight

1 Electricity can be generated from fossil fuels in power stations.

Explain how turbines and electrical generators are used to generate electricity from fossil fuels.

....

....

....

....

....

[Total 4 marks]

2 Oil and plutonium can be used as energy resources. Plutonium is a nuclear fuel. One of the drawbacks of using oil and plutonium is that they are non-renewable energy resources.

a) Explain what is meant by a non-renewable energy resource.

....

[1]

b) Explain **two** other drawbacks of using oil as an energy resource.

....

....

....

....

....

[4]

c) Give **one** drawback of using plutonium as an energy resource instead of oil.

....

....

[1]

[Total 6 marks]

Renewable Energy Resources

1 Tidal barrages use water to generate electricity.

a) Which of the following statements about tidal barrages is true?
Place a tick (✓) in the box next to the statement that is true.

They generate the same amount of electricity all the time. ☐

They are usually built on top of hills. ☐

They can disturb the habitats of animals. ☐

They produce pollution when generating electricity. ☐

[1]

b) Hydroelectric power plants also use water to generate electricity.
Give **one** advantage of generating electricity using
hydroelectric power plants instead of tidal barrages.

....

....

[1]

[Total 2 marks]

2 Wind turbines use wind power to generate electricity.

a) Describe how wind turbines generate electricity.

....

....

....

[2]

b) Suraj is discussing wind turbines. He makes the following statement:

> **Suraj**
> Wind turbines are a great way to produce
> electricity. They don't cause any pollution
> and they can produce electricity all the time.

Explain why Suraj's statement is partly right, and partly wrong.

....

....

....

....

[2]

[Total 4 marks]

3 A university wants to reduce their energy bills. They want to build either a single wind turbine nearby, or install solar panels on top of their buildings.

The average wind speed for the university the previous year is shown in the table below. The average number of hours of sunlight per day is also given.

	Average wind speed (m/s)	Average number of hours of daylight
October-March	8.0	9
April-September	4.3	15

The university decides to install both a wind turbine and solar panels.
Use the information in the table to suggest why.

....

....

....

....

....

....

....

....

[Total 4 marks]

4* Fossil fuels are the most common way to fuel a car. Some modern cars use biofuels.

Discuss the benefits and drawbacks of using biofuels to fuel a car.
Compare these benefits and drawbacks to using fossil fuels in cars.

....

....

....

....

....

....

....

....

....

[Total 6 marks]

Trends in Energy Use

1 The diagram below shows the energy resources used to generate electricity in a country.

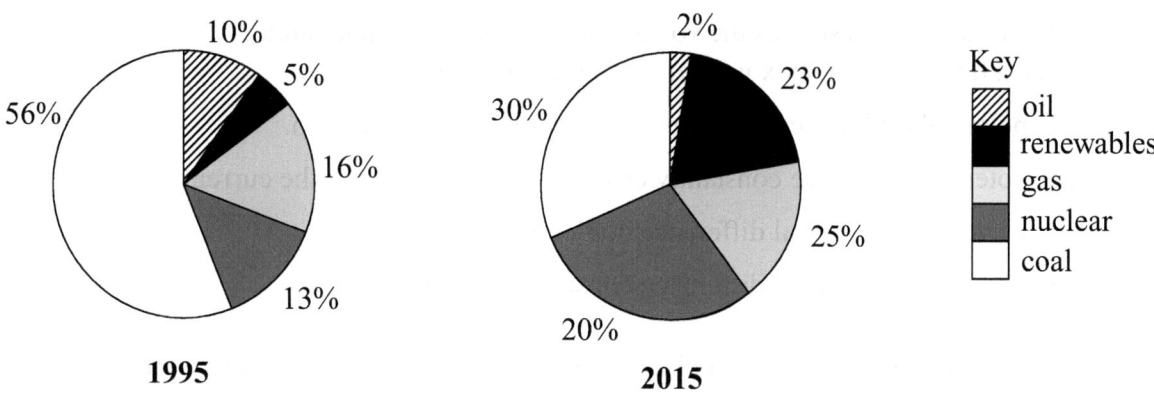

1995   **2015**

a) Determine what percentage of the country's electricity was generated by fossil fuels in 1995.

.... %
[2]

b) Suggest **one** trend you can determine from the pie charts in the diagram.

....

....
[1]
[Total 3 marks]

2 In the UK, the use of renewable energy resources is increasing.

a) State and explain **one** possible reason for this increase in the use of renewable energy resources.

....

....

....
[2]

b)* Discuss the factors which may reduce the rate at which we decrease our use of fossil fuels and increase our use of renewable energy resources.

....

....

....

....

....

....

....
[6]
[Total 8 marks]

The National Grid

1 The UK mains supplies an alternating voltage to a telephone that is turned on.

a) Which statement describes the voltage and current in the telephone?
Place a tick (✓) in the box next to the correct answer.

The potential difference and current constantly change direction. ☐

The potential difference constantly changes direction, but not the current. ☐

The current and potential difference don't change direction. ☐

The current and potential difference constantly switch on and off. ☐

[1]

b) State the potential difference and frequency of the UK mains electricity. State the units.

Potential difference: .... Frequency: ....

[1]

[Total 2 marks]

2 Complete the following table to show whether each statement about the national grid is **true** or **false**. Place a tick (✓) in the correct boxes.

Statement	True	False
Transformers increase the size of the electrical current before it is transferred through the national grid.		
Transferring electricity through the national grid at high p.d. reduces energy loss.		
Transformers decrease the p.d. of electricity from the national grid before it reaches homes and businesses.		

[Total 2 marks]

3 The cable that connects an iron to the mains supply has become worn with use. The live wire is now exposed.

a) Tim plugs in the iron and switches it on. The electric potential of Tim is 0 V. What will happen if Tim accidentally touches the live wire? Explain your answer.

....

....

....

....

[3]

b) The cable for the iron also contains an earth wire. Explain the function of the earth wire.

....

....

[1]

[Total 4 marks]

Chapter P2 — Sustainable Energy

Chapter P3 — Electric Circuits

Current, Potential Difference and Resistance

Warm-Up

Draw a line to match each variable on the left to its unit name and symbol on the right.

potential difference	ampere, A
current	ohm, Ω
charge	volt, V
resistance	coulomb, C

1 A simple circuit that contains a resistor is shown on the right. *Grade 3-4*

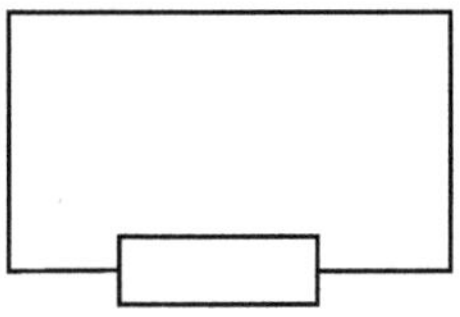

a) Explain why there is no current in the circuit.

....
[1]

b) Use the correct phrase from the box below to complete the sentence.

| electrical charge | potential difference | resistance | frequency |

Current is the rate of flow of ....

.... is anything which slows down this flow.

[2]
[Total 3 marks]

2 A charge of 420 C flows through a filament lamp in 120 seconds. *Grade 4-5*

a) State the equation that links current, charge and time.

....
[1]

b) Calculate the current flowing through the lamp.

Current = ... A
[3]
[Total 4 marks]

Describing and Drawing Circuits

Warm-Up

Draw lines to match each circuit symbol to its correct name.

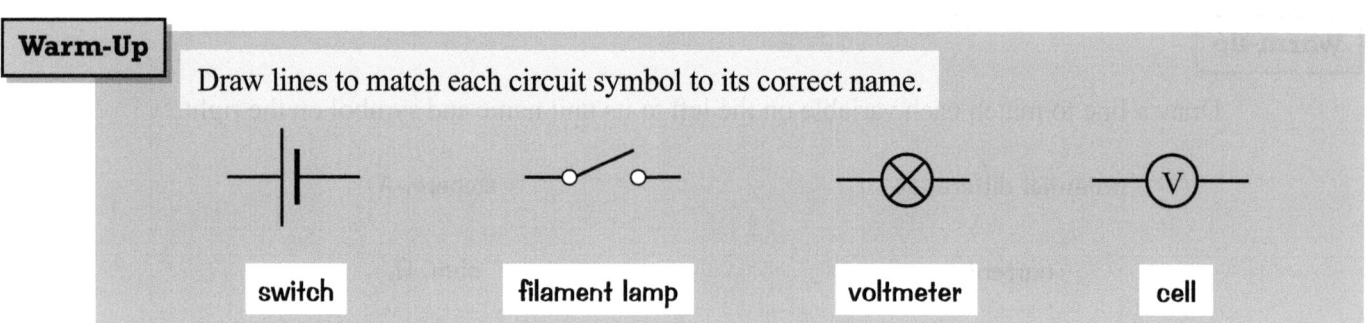

1   A current of 3 A flows through a 6 Ω resistor.

   Calculate the potential difference across the resistor.
   Use the equation:

   $$\text{potential difference} = \text{current} \times \text{resistance}$$

   Potential difference = ...V
   [Total 2 marks]

2   The figure below shows the circuit symbol for a variable resistor.

   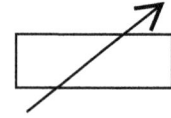

   a) Draw a circuit diagram of a circuit made up of a cell, a filament lamp and a variable resistor, connected on a single, closed loop of wire.

   [3]

   b) The variable resistor can be used to change the resistance of the circuit. Explain how increasing the resistance of the variable resistor will affect the current through the circuit.

   ....

   ....
   [2]
   [Total 5 marks]

Chapter P3 — Electric Circuits

Investigating Resistance

PRACTICAL

1   Jackie investigated how the resistance of a piece of wire depends on its length. The circuit she used is shown below. Her results are displayed in the table on the right.

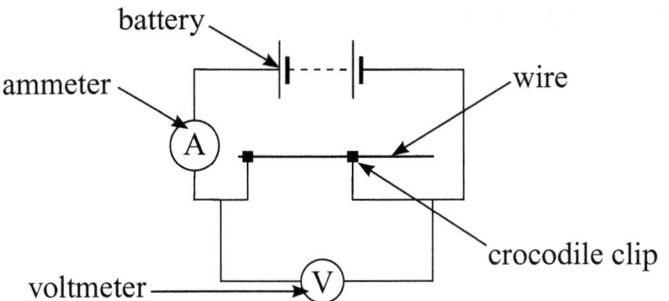

Length / cm	Resistance / Ω
10	0.6
20	1.2
30	1.8
40	2.4
50	3.0

a) Describe how Jackie could have used the apparatus above to obtain her results.

....

....

....
[2]

b) Complete the graph below, by plotting the remaining data points from the table. Draw a line of best fit on the graph.

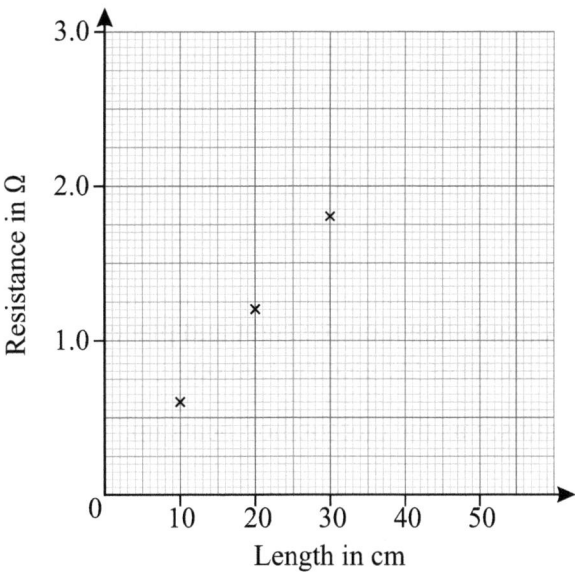

[2]

c) What does the graph show? Place a tick (✓) in the box next to the correct answer.

Resistance is directly proportional to length. ☐

There is no relationship between resistance and length. ☐

Resistance is inversely proportional to length. ☐

Resistance increases with length up to a point, and then starts decreasing. ☐

[1]

[Total 5 marks]

Chapter P3 — Electric Circuits

LDRs and Thermistors

1 Sophia wants to investigate how the resistance of an LDR changes with light intensity.

a) Draw a circuit diagram (including an ammeter and a voltmeter) of a circuit that could be used to measure the resistance of an LDR.

[3]

b) Sophia varies the intensity of the light hitting the LDR by partly covering it with a piece of paper. She covers the LDR with the paper by varying amounts, and calculates the resistance each time. Her results are shown in the table below.

Percentage of resistor covered	Resistance (Ω)
0%	800
25%	1000
50%	1300
75%	1800

Describe what Sophia's results show about the relationship between the light intensity the LDR is exposed to and its resistance.

....

....

[1]
[Total 4 marks]

2 Mark builds the sensing circuit shown on the right and places it next to an electric hob. He turns the electric hob on.

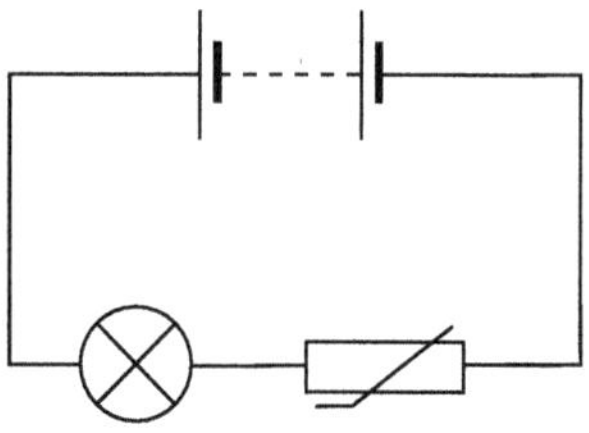

Describe what Mark would see as the electric hob heats up. Explain this observation.

....

....

....

....

....

[Total 4 marks]

I-V Characteristics

1 Electrical components can be linear or non-linear.

a) Which of the graphs below is an *I-V* characteristic of a linear component?
Place a tick (✓) in the box next to the correct answer.

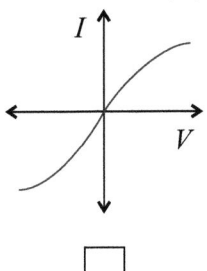 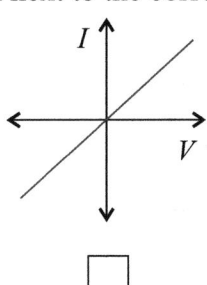 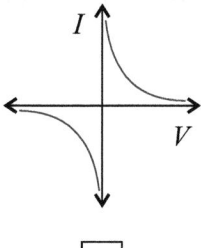 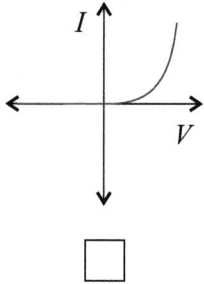

☐ ☐ ☐ ☐

[1]

b) Give **one** example of a linear component.

....

[1]

[Total 2 marks]

2 Gita is investigating the *I-V* characteristic of a filament lamp. She uses the circuit shown on the right.

a) Describe a method Gita could use to determine the *I-V* characteristic of the filament lamp.

....

....

....

....

....

....

[3]

b) The graph on the right shows the *I-V* characteristic plotted from her results. Using the graph, calculate the resistance of the filament lamp when the current through it is 2.0 A.

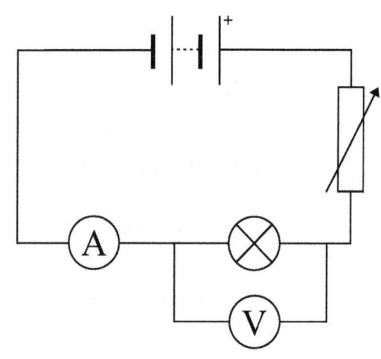

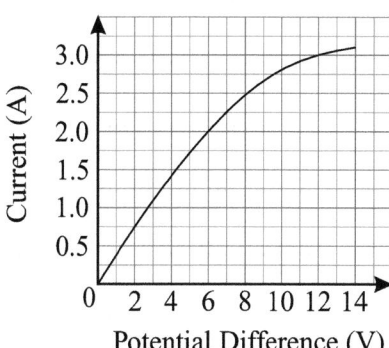

Resistance = ... Ω

[4]

[Total 7 marks]

Chapter P3 — Electric Circuits

Circuit Devices and *I-V* Characteristics

1 The diagram on the right shows the *I-V* characteristic of a diode.

a) Using the graph, describe how the current through the diode changes with potential difference.

....

....

....

....
[3]

b) Diodes can be used to change an alternating current into a direct current. Suggest why diodes are suited to this use.

....

....
[1]
[Total 4 marks]

2* The diagram on the right shows the *I-V* characteristic of a thermistor in a room at a constant temperature.

Explain the shape of the thermistor's *I-V* characteristic.

....

....

....

....

....

....

....

....

....

....

....
[Total 6 marks]

Chapter P3 — Electric Circuits

Energy in Circuits

1. The power supply for a remote-controlled car is a battery.

    Which of the following is the main energy transfer from the battery to the toy car?
    Place a tick (✓) in the box next to the correct answer.

    By heating to the electrostatic energy store of the car's motor. ☐

    Electrically to the nuclear energy store of the car's motor. ☐

    Electrically to the kinetic energy store of the car's motor. ☐

    Mechanically to the elastic potential energy store of the car's motor. ☐

    [Total 1 mark]

2. A kettle does a total of 552 000 J of work to bring water to the boil. It is connected to a power supply that provides a potential difference of 230 V and causes a current to flow in the kettle's electrical circuit.

    a) State what the potential difference between two points in the circuit measures.

    ....

    ....
    [1]

    b) Calculate the total charge that passes through the kettle in the time it takes to boil the water.
    Use the equation:

    $$\text{potential difference} = \text{work done} \div \text{charge}$$

    Charge = ... C
    [3]

    c) A toaster is connected to the same power supply. During the time it takes to toast a slice of bread, the total charge that passes through the toaster is 1300 C.

    Calculate the energy transferred by the toaster in this time.
    Give your answer in kilojoules.

    Energy transferred = ... kJ
    [3]

    [Total 7 marks]

Exam Practice Tip

Remember the difference between the potential difference across power supplies and across components. For power supplies, it's the work done *to* each unit of charge. For a component, its the work done *by* each unit of charge.

Chapter P3 — Electric Circuits

Series Circuits

1 Three circuits are shown below. One of the circuits has all of its components connected in series. Place a tick (✓) in the box next to the correct answer.

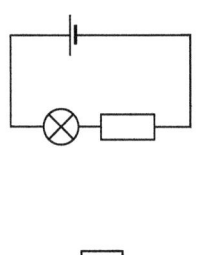 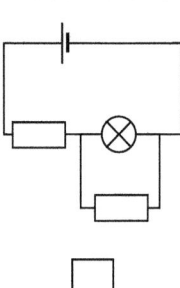 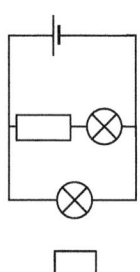 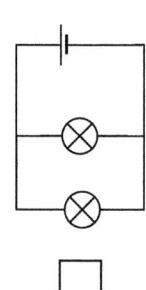

☐ ☐ ☐ ☐

[Total 1 mark]

2 The diagram on the right shows a circuit containing two resistors connected in series.

a) What is the total resistance of the circuit?
Draw a circle around the correct answer.

10 Ω   30 Ω   20 Ω   60 Ω

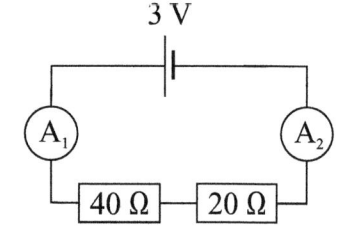

[1]

b) The reading on ammeter A_1 in the circuit is 0.05 A.
Write down the reading on ammeter A_2.

Current = ... A
[1]

c) A third resistor is added in series to the circuit.
The potential difference across the 40 Ω resistor is 1.2 V.
The potential difference across the 20 Ω resistor is 0.6 V.
Calculate the potential difference across the third resistor.

Potential difference = ... V
[2]
[Total 4 marks]

Exam Practice Tip

Ammeters and voltmeters have to be connected in a certain way, no matter what type of circuit you are making. A voltmeter must always be connected in parallel with what you're measuring the potential difference across. But the circuit will still count as a series circuit if everything else is connected around one loop of wire.

Parallel Circuits

Warm-Up

In the circuit diagram below, which filament lamp is connected in parallel with the resistor? Tick (✓) **one** box.

A ☐
B ☐
C ☐

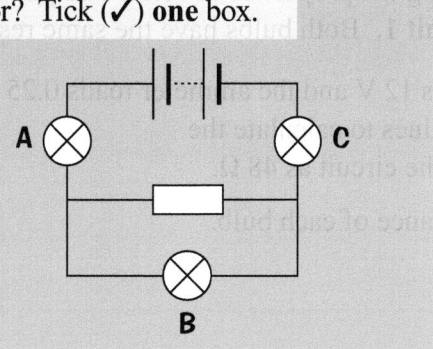

1   The circuit on the right is a parallel circuit containing two resistors, R_1 and R_2.

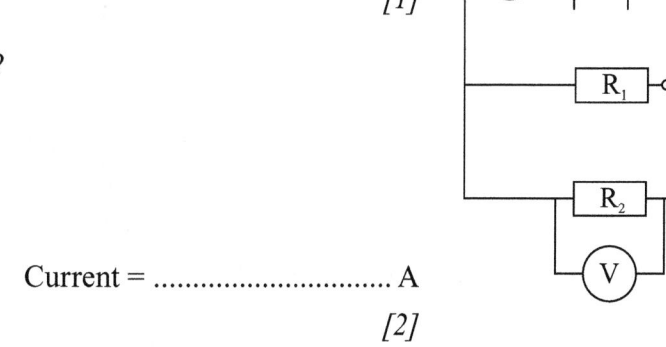

a) The current through R_1 is 4 A. The current through R_2 is 2 A.

i) Which resistor has the highest resistance?

....
[1]

ii) What is the reading on the ammeter?

Current = ... A
[2]

b) What is the reading on the voltmeter?

Potential difference = ... V
[1]

c) The switch is now opened, as shown in the circuit on the right. Which of the following statements about the total resistance of the circuit is **true**? Place a tick (✓) in the box next to the correct answer.

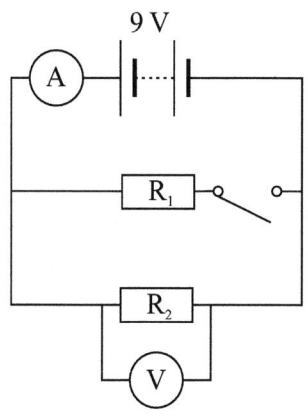

The total resistance is higher when the switch is open. ☐

The total resistance is lower when the switch is open. ☐

The total resistance does not change when the switch is opened. ☐

The total resistance is zero when the switch is open. ☐

[1]

[Total 5 marks]

Chapter P3 — Electric Circuits

Investigating Series and Parallel Circuits

PRACTICAL

1 Doris is investigating the properties of series and parallel circuits. Doris sets up **Circuit 1**. Both bulbs have the same resistance.

The voltmeter reads 12 V and the ammeter reads 0.25 A. Doris uses these values to calculate the total resistance of the circuit as 48 Ω.

Circuit 1

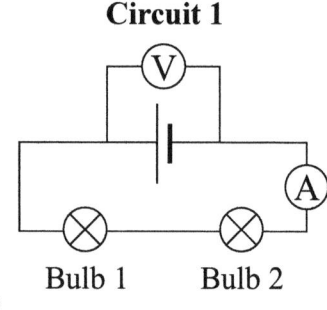

a) Calculate the resistance of each bulb.

Resistance = ... Ω
[1]

b) Doris then adds Bulb 3, as shown in **Circuit 2**. Bulb 3 is identical to Bulbs 1 and 2.

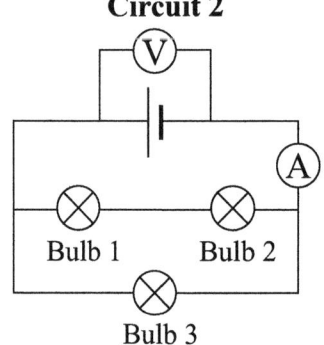

i) Calculate the current through Bulb 3.

Current through Bulb 3 = ... A
[3]

ii) Doris observes that Bulb 3 is brighter than Bulbs 1 and 2. Explain why.

....
....
....
[2]

c) Doris then adds a resistor to the circuit, in series with Bulb 3, as shown in **Circuit 3**. State how this affects the brightness of the three bulbs.

Circuit 3

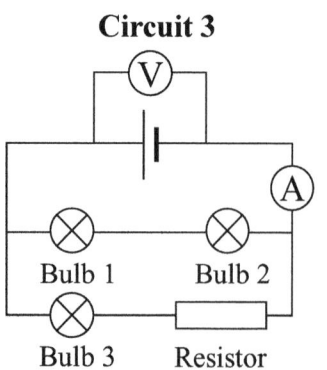

....
....
[2]

[Total 8 marks]

Electrical Power

Warm-Up

For each statement, circle whether it is true or false.

Power is the total amount of work done by an electrical appliance.	True / False
The units of power are J/N.	True / False
Power in an electrical circuit depends on the current and potential difference.	True / False

1 An electric heater has a potential difference of 230 V and a current of 2.80 A. It is used to heat a beaker of water.

Calculate the power of the heater.

Power = ... W

[Total 3 marks]

2 A circuit component has a power rating of 0.015 kW.

a) What is meant by the power rating of a circuit component?

....

[1]

b) Calculate the energy transferred to the component when operating at its power rating for 10.0 hours. Give your answer in joules.
Use the equation:

$$\text{power} = \text{energy transferred} \div \text{time}$$

Energy transferred = ... J

[4]

c) The current through the component is 5 A. Calculate the resistance of the component.
Use the equation:

$$\text{power} = (\text{current})^2 \times \text{resistance}$$

Resistance = ... Ω

[3]

[Total 8 marks]

Chapter P3 — Electric Circuits

Transformers

Warm-Up

Use the words given below to label the diagram.

cables   power station   step-up transformer   step-down transformer

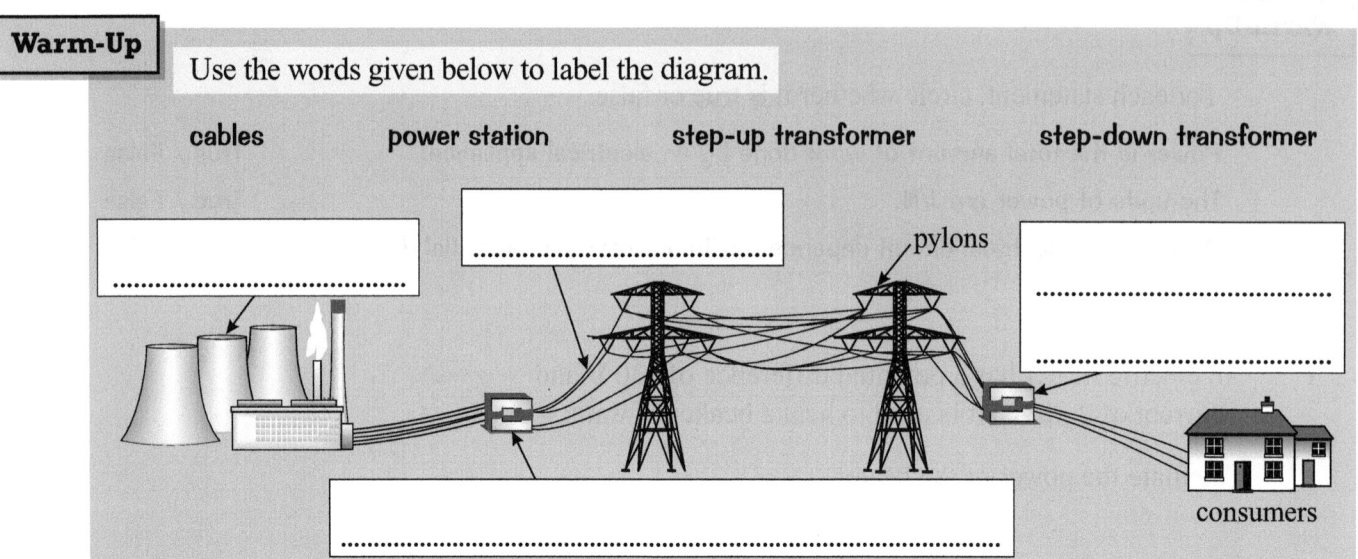

1   The diagram below shows a step-up transformer in a wind farm. The transformer changes the potential difference generated by the wind farm from 12 000 V to 400 000 V.

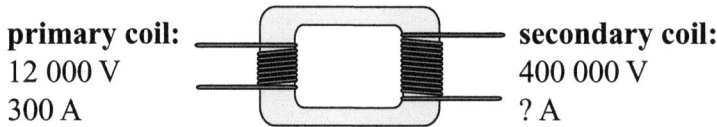

Calculate the current in the secondary coil of the transformer.
Use the correct equation from the Physics Equation Sheet.

Current = ... A
[Total 3 marks]

2   The national grid has to transfer a lot of energy.
Explain how the national grid transfers this energy efficiently.

....
....
....
....
....

[Total 3 marks]

Chapter P3 — Electric Circuits

Permanent and Induced Magnets

1 Zoey is investigating the magnetic field around a bar magnet. *(Grade 3-4)*

a) What is meant by the term magnetic field?

....

....
[1]

Magnetic fields can be represented by field lines. Zoey draws the diagram below to show the magnetic field lines around a bar magnet. The diagram is incomplete.

b) Complete the diagram by drawing arrows on the field lines to show their direction.
[1]

c) Another magnet is brought near the bar magnet, so that the south poles of each magnet are close to each other. This causes each magnet to move. State how the magnets move. Explain why this happens.

....

....
[2]

[Total 4 marks]

2 The diagram below shows the magnetic field pattern around a permanent bar magnet, and a bar of iron. *(Grade 4-5)*

a) Explain why there is a magnetic field pattern around the iron bar.

....

....
[2]

b) State what happens to the magnetic field around the iron bar when the bar magnet is removed.

....
[1]

[Total 3 marks]

Magnetism and Electromagnetism

1 Monica is researching how magnetic compasses are used for navigation. The needle of a compass is a small bar magnet. The north pole of the needle of a compass always points north when not near another magnet.

Monica makes the following statement:

Monica
The fact that the compass needle points north is evidence that the Earth's core is magnetic.

Explain why Monica's statement is correct.

....

....

....

....

[Total 3 marks]

2 The diagram below shows a current-carrying wire and the magnetic field pattern around it. Three points are labelled **X**, **Y** and **Z**.

a) Draw an arrow on the current-carrying wire to show the direction of the current.
[1]

b) State at which point, **X**, **Y** or **Z**, the magnetic field is strongest.

....
[1]

c) The wire above is carrying a current of 0.5 A. A second wire is carrying a current of 0.2 A. Explain which wire has the strongest magnetic field around it.

....

....

[2]

[Total 4 marks]

Exam Practice Tip
Use your right hand to find the magnetic field direction around a current-carrying wire. Stick your thumb in the direction of the current and curl your fingers — they will be pointing in the direction of the field lines round the wire.

Chapter P3 — Electric Circuits

Solenoids and Electromagnets

1 Use phrases from the box below to complete the passage below.

| add together | weaker | stronger | multiply | cancel out |

When a straight current-carrying wire is wound into a solenoid, the

magnetic field lines of the current-carrying wire ....

This produces a magnetic field that is ....

than the field along the straight current-carrying wire.

[Total 2 marks]

2 The diagram below shows a solenoid carrying a current. A magnetic field is produced inside and around the solenoid.

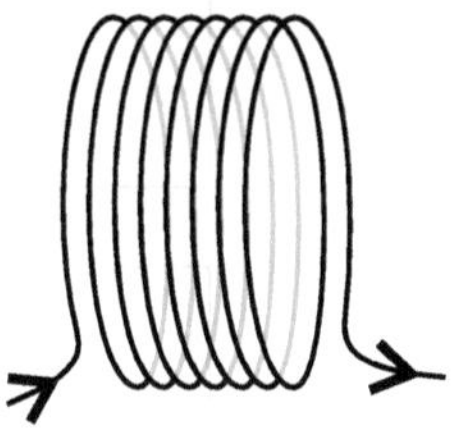

a) The three changes listed below are made to the solenoid.
What happens to the magnetic field of the solenoid in each case?
Place a tick (✓) in the box next to the correct answer for each change.

	It gets stronger	It gets weaker	It reverses
Change 1: The current is reversed.	☐	☐	☐
Change 2: An iron core is placed in the centre of the solenoid.	☐	☐	☐
Change 3: The length of the solenoid is kept constant, but the number of turns is decreased.	☐	☐	☐

[3]

b) What is the solenoid known as once an iron core has been added to the centre?

....

[1]

c) Suggest a possible use for a solenoid with an iron core in the centre.

....

[1]

[Total 5 marks]

Chapter P4 — Explaining Motion

Forces and Newton's Third Law

1 The diagram shows skater A pushing on skater B with a force of 100 N. Using Newton's Third Law, what force does skater B exert on skater A? Place a tick (✓) in the box next to the correct answer.

50 N ☐

150 N ☐

200 N ☐

100 N ☐

[Total 1 mark]

2 Draw straight lines to match each force on the left to its correct description on the right.

| Friction | | Acts between all objects that are touching each other. |

| Normal contact force | | Acts between charges when their electric fields interact. |

| Electrostatic force | | Acts between objects that are touching and trying to slide past each other. |

[Total 2 marks]

3 Dave is at rest on his skateboard next to a wall. You can assume there is no friction between the skateboard and the ground.

Dave makes the following statement:

Dave: If I push on the wall, I will move away from the wall.

Explain why Dave's statement is correct.

....

....

....

....

[Total 2 marks]

Mass and Weight

Warm-Up

State whether each of the following statements are true or false.

1) Weight is a force caused by gravity. ....

2) Weight is always an upwards force. ....

3) Weight can be measured using a voltmeter. ....

1 Which of the following statements correctly describes the relationship between the mass of an object and its weight? Place a tick (✓) in the box next to the correct answer.

The larger the mass of an object, the smaller its weight. ☐

The larger the mass of an object, the larger its weight. ☐

The mass of an object is equal to its weight. ☐

There is no relationship between the mass of an object and its weight. ☐

[Total 1 mark]

2 The Opportunity rover is a 185 kg robot. It was made on Earth and sent to the surface of the planet Mars.

a) State the equation that links weight, mass and gravitational field strength.

....
[1]

b) Calculate the weight of Opportunity when it was on Earth.
(The gravitational field strength on the surface of Earth = 10 N/kg.)

Weight = ... N
[2]

c) The weight of Opportunity on Mars is 703 N.
Calculate the gravitational field strength on the surface of Mars.

Gravitational field strength = ... N/kg
[3]

[Total 6 marks]

Exam Practice Tip

If you're struggling to remember an equation, looking at the units of the values you've been given might help you. If the units include a slash (like N/kg), it shows that something must be divided by something else to get that value.

Chapter P4 — Explaining Motion

Distance, Displacement, Speed and Velocity

Warm-Up

Write each word below in the table on the right to show whether it is a scalar or vector quantity.

displacement   velocity   speed   distance   force

Scalar	Vector

1 The diagram below shows the path taken by a football kicked by a child. When it is kicked at point A, the ball moves horizontally to the right until it hits a vertical wall at point B. The ball then bounces back horizontally to the left and comes to rest at point C.

A   C   B   Scale 1 cm = 1 m

a) What is the total distance travelled by the ball as it moves from A to B?

Distance = ... m
[1]

b) Calculate the total distance travelled by the ball after it has come to rest.

Distance = ... m
[1]

c) What is the displacement of the ball after it has come to rest?

Displacement = ... m to the ....
[2]

[Total 4 marks]

2 Cecil walks 2.1 km to his work place. Estimate how long his journey takes, using your knowledge of typical speeds.

Use the equation:

average speed = distance ÷ time

Time taken = ... s
[Total 4 marks]

Chapter P4 — Explaining Motion

Measuring and Converting Units

1 A car travels down a motorway.

a) The car is on the motorway for 2 hours.
Calculate this time in milliseconds.

Time = ... ms
[2]

b) The car is travelling at a speed of 90 km/h.
Calculate its speed in m/s.

Speed = ... m/s
[2]

[Total 4 marks]

2 Justin and Sydney are designing an experiment to measure the speed of a remote control car travelling 1.5 m. To do this, they need to measure the distance the car will travel and the time taken for the car to travel this distance.

Justin and Sydney have different ideas about how to take the measurements.

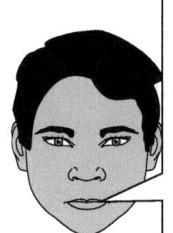

Justin
We should measure the time with light gates, and measure the distance with a 30 cm ruler.

Sydney
We should measure the time with a stopwatch, and measure the distance with a 2 m tape measure.

Discuss how sensible Justin and Sydney's suggestions for measuring time and speed are.

....
....
....
....
....
....

[Total 4 marks]

Chapter P4 — Explaining Motion

Acceleration

1 A car undergoes uniform acceleration from rest. It reaches a speed of 12 m/s in 3 s.

Calculate the acceleration of the car.
Use the equation:
$$\text{acceleration} = \text{change in speed} \div \text{time taken}$$

Acceleration = ... m/s²
[Total 3 marks]

2 A train is travelling at 18 m/s. It accelerates uniformly to a speed of 32 m/s over a distance of 350 m. Calculate the acceleration of the train over this distance. Use an equation from the Equations List.

Acceleration = ... m/s²
[Total 3 marks]

3 Rachael is running in a race. After she crosses the finish line, she takes 5 s to decelerate from a typical running speed to a speed of 0.5 m/s.

Estimate Rachael's deceleration after she crosses the finish line.

Deceleration = – (minus) .... m/s²
[Total 4 marks]

Exam Practice Tip
There are two equations for acceleration that you need to know how and when to use. Making a list of the information you're given can help — whether you are given 'distance' or 'time' should give you a clue as to which equation to use.

Chapter P4 — Explaining Motion

Investigating Motion PRACTICAL

1   Alice wants to carry out an experiment to investigate the motion of a trolley down a ramp. Her textbook suggests setting up her apparatus as shown in the diagram.

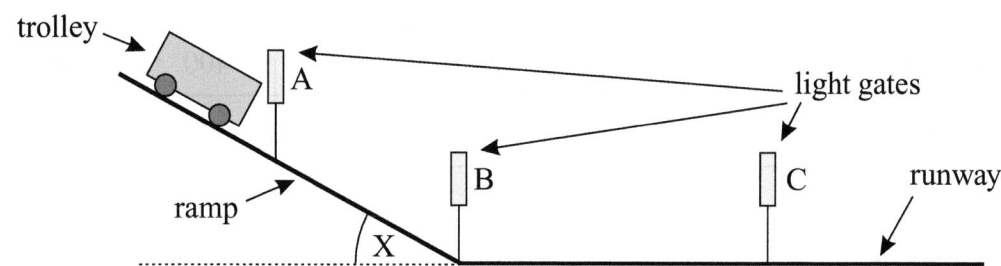

a)* Describe how Alice could use this apparatus to find the acceleration of the trolley down the ramp.

....
....
....
....
....
....
....
....
....
....
....
....

[6]

b) What would happen to the speed of the trolley on the runway if the angle labelled X in the diagram was increased?

....

[1]

c) The ramp is changed so that its surface is covered with carpet. There is now more friction between the trolley and the ramp. What happens to the speed of the trolley on the runway?

....

[1]

[Total 8 marks]

Chapter P4 — Explaining Motion

Distance-Time Graphs

1. A motor boat is travelling along a straight canal. Some students time how long it takes the boat to pass markers spaced 100 metres apart. The table shows their results. The grid shows an incomplete distance-time graph for the boat.

Distance (m)	0	100	200	300	400	500
Time (s)	0	85	170	255	340	425

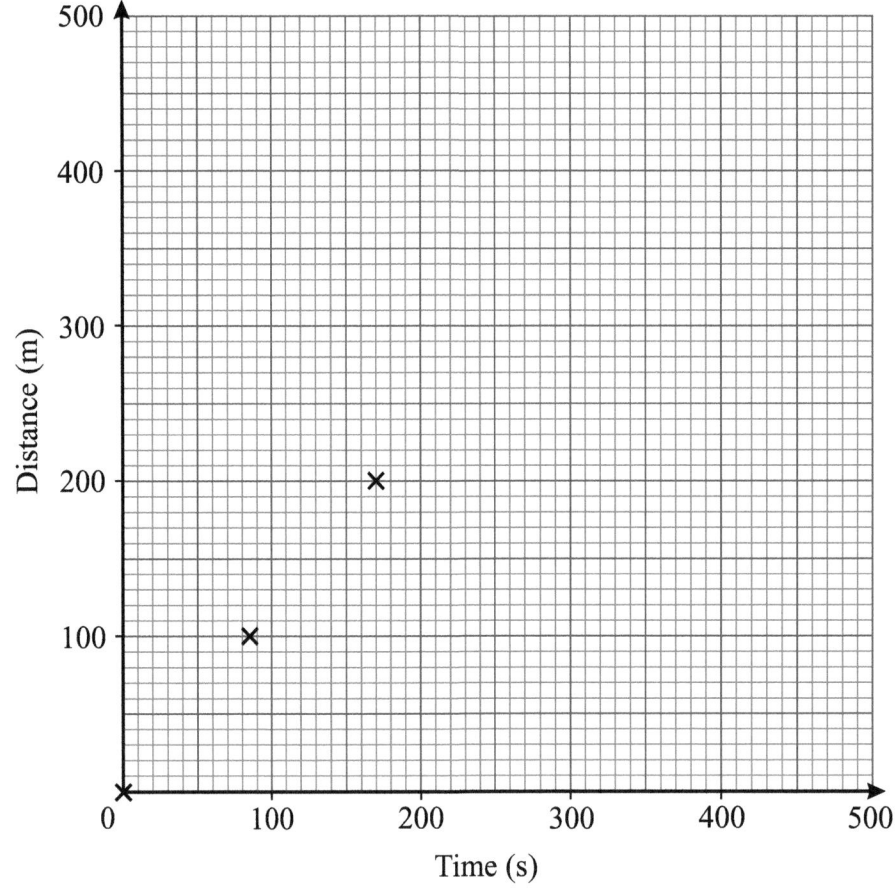

a) Complete the distance-time graph using the results in the table.
[2]

b) Using the graph, estimate how far the boat travelled in 300 s.

Distance = ... m
[1]

c) Using the graph, estimate how long it took the boat to travel 250 m.

Time = ... s
[1]

d) Describe the boat's speed during the first 500 m of its journey.

....
[1]

[Total 5 marks]

Chapter P4 — Explaining Motion

Velocity-Time Graphs

Warm-Up

Use two of the phrases from the list below to correctly label the speed-time graph.

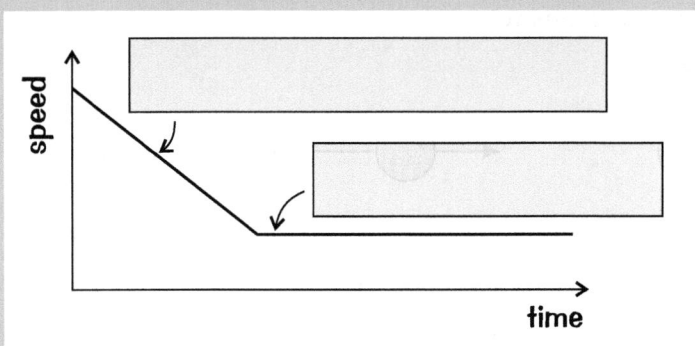

decreasing deceleration

steady speed

decreasing acceleration

constant acceleration

constant deceleration

1 The graph below shows a velocity-time graph for a roller coaster car travelling in a straight line.

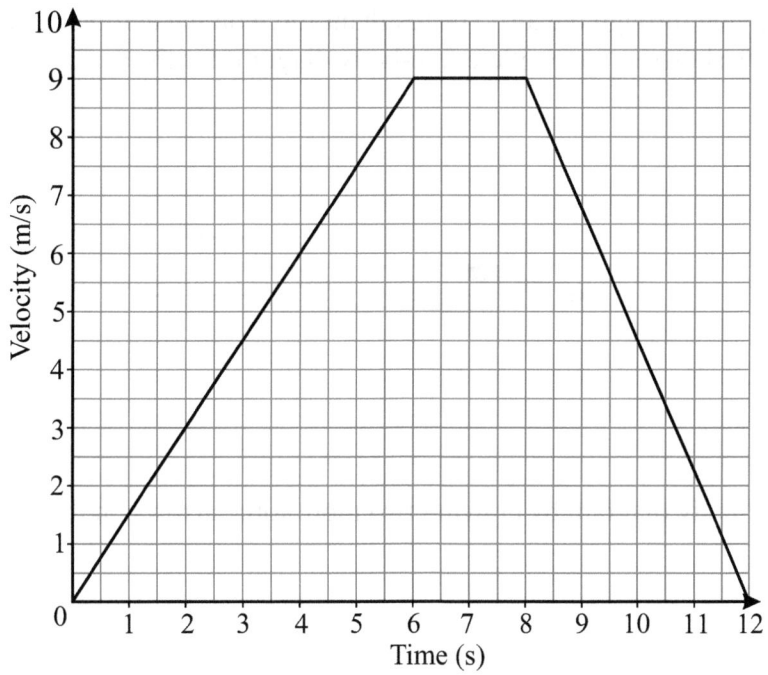

a) Using the graph, calculate the acceleration for the car between 0 s and 6 s.

Acceleration = ... m/s²
[2]

b) Calculate the distance travelled by the car while it is travelling at a constant speed.

Distance travelled = ... m
[2]

[Total 4 marks]

Chapter P4 — Explaining Motion

Free Body Diagrams and Resultant Forces

1 The free body diagrams for four rubber balls are shown below.

Which diagram shows a rubber ball with a non-zero resultant force acting on it?
Place a tick (✓) in the box below the correct answer.

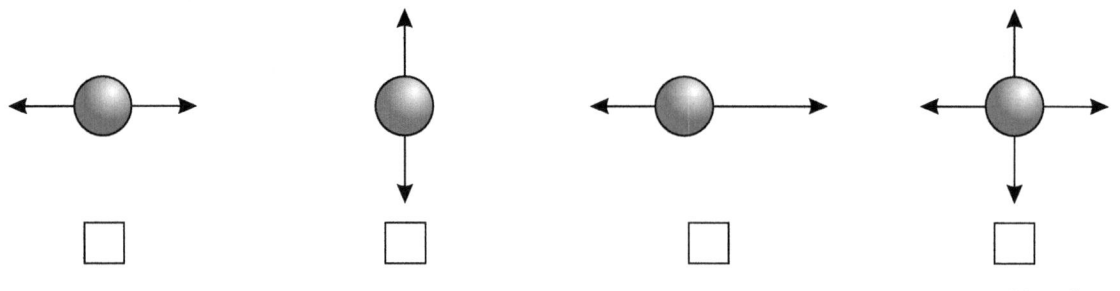

□   □   □   □

[Total 1 mark]

2 An aeroplane is flying through the air. The resultant force on the aeroplane is zero.
The diagram below shows an incomplete free-body diagram for the aeroplane.

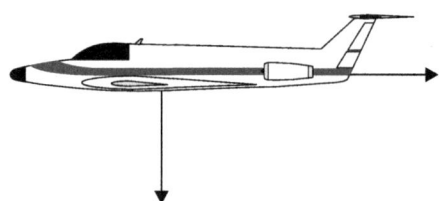

Complete the free-body diagram by drawing two more force arrows on the diagram.

[Total 3 marks]

3 A toy car is at rest on a table. A free body force diagram of the car is shown on the right.

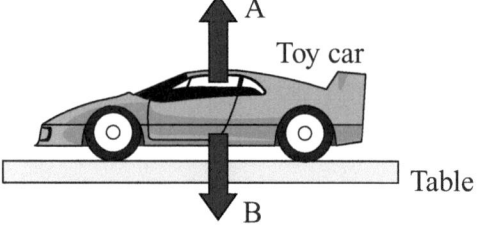

a) Name the forces that are labelled A and B in the diagram.

A = ...

B = ...

[2]

b) Someone pushes the car so there is a resultant force towards the left and it starts to move.
Draw and label arrows on the diagram to show the new forces acting on the car.

[3]

[Total 5 marks]

Chapter P4 — Explaining Motion

Newton's First and Second Laws

1 A space shuttle is travelling through space. It turns on its thrusters, which produces a resultant force in the direction shown on the diagram below.

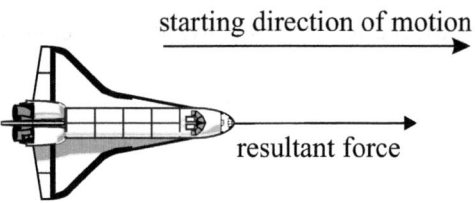

Which of the following statements correctly describes how the motion of the shuttle changes due to the resultant force? Place a tick (✓) in the box next to the correct answer.

The shuttle's speed increases, but its direction of motion stays the same. ☐

The shuttle's speed stays the same, but its direction of motion changes. ☐

The shuttle's speed increases and its direction of motion changes. ☐

The shuttle's speed and direction of motion stay the same. ☐

[Total 1 mark]

2 Complete the statement of Newton's First Law using phrases from the box below.

| increase | gravitational | decrease | stay the same | resultant |

Newton's First Law states that if the .... force acting

on a moving object is zero, the velocity of the object will ....

If the force is non-zero and acts in the opposite direction to the movement of the object,

the velocity of the object will ....

[Total 3 marks]

3 The diagram below shows an accelerating motorbike. It shows the resultant force acting on the motorbike. The motorbike and rider have a combined mass of 400 kg.

Calculate the acceleration of the motorbike. Give the correct units.

Acceleration = ... Unit = ...

[Total 5 marks]

Chapter P4 — Explaining Motion

Reaction Times

1 A teacher tests the reaction times of three of her students.
   She measures how far a ruler vertically falls before the student catches it.

   a) Explain why it would not be suitable to use a stopwatch to measure a student's reaction time.

   ....
   [1]

   The table below shows the teacher's results.
   The values in the table show the distance the ruler falls in centimetres during each attempt.

	Attempt 1 (cm)	Attempt 2 (cm)	Attempt 3 (cm)	Average (cm)
Student A	27.0	27.1	26.9	27.0
Student B	28.4	28.2	28.3	28.3
Student C	26.5	27.0	26.0	26.5

   b) State which student has the fastest average reaction time. Explain your answer.

   ....

   ....
   [2]

   c) Give **two** ways the teacher could make the experiment a fair test.

   ....

   ....
   [2]

   d) The teacher repeats the experiment.
      This time, she has someone talk to each student while they are being tested.
      Describe how you would expect this to affect the reaction times of the students.

   ....
   [1]

   e) A fourth student, Student D, tests his reaction time using the same method as the teacher.
      He calculates his reaction time as 4.5 s.
      Explain how you know Student D has made an error in his experiment.

   ....

   ....
   [1]

   [Total 7 marks]

Exam Practice Tip

Make sure you know the ruler drop experiment really well. You could be ask to fully describe the method on the exam, as well as being asked about the results, so make sure you've got the key steps firmly in your brain.

Stopping Distances

Warm-Up

Circle the factors below which affect the braking distance of a vehicle.

Drinking alcohol   Broken headlights   Mass of the vehicle

Bald tyres   Drug use
            Driver distractions
     Faulty brakes   Speed of the vehicle

1   The stopping distance of a vehicle depends on the driver's reaction distance.

   a) What is meant by the term 'reaction distance'?

   ....
   [1]

   b) State the effect drinking alcohol would have on a driver's reaction distance. Explain your answer.

   ....
   ....
   [2]

   c) State **one** other factor which can affect a driver's reaction distance.

   ....
   [1]
   [Total 4 marks]

2   A car is travelling along a flat road and has to stop in an emergency. Its braking distance is 18 m.

   a) What is meant by the term 'braking distance'?

   ....
   [1]

   b) The car travels down the same road the next day. There is ice on the road.
      Explain how the braking distance of the car would be affected by the change in conditions.

   ....
   ....
   ....
   [2]
   [Total 3 marks]

Vehicle Safety

1 Jack finds the graph shown below in a science book. The graph shows how the force on passengers in a car changes with the time taken for the car to slow down from 30 m/s to rest.

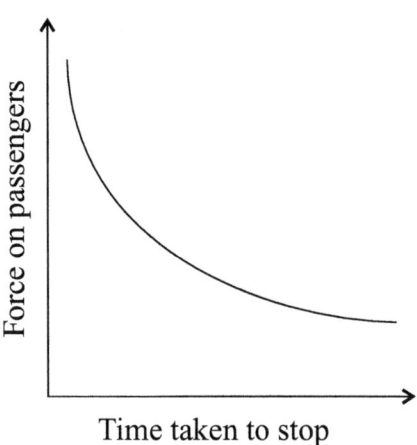

State **one** conclusion Jack could make from this graph.

....

....

[Total 1 mark]

2 All modern cars are fitted with air bags as a safety feature.

a) Explain how air bags protect drivers and passengers from injury during a car crash. You should use ideas about forces and deceleration in your answer.

....

....

....

....

....

....

....

[4]

b) Name **one** other safety feature a modern car will have to help protect the driver and passengers in a crash.

....

[1]

[Total 5 marks]

Work Done and Power

1 A student does 150 Nm of work pushing a trolley. *Grade 1-3*

How many joules of energy are transferred to the trolley?
Place a tick (✓) in the box next to the correct answer.

50 J ☐

100 J ☐

150 J ☐

300 J ☐

[Total 1 mark]

2 A man lifts a box of books 150 cm vertically using a force of 60 N. *Grade 3-4*

Calculate the work done on the box of books.

Work done = ... J
[Total 4 marks]

3 A student heats a beaker of water using an immersion heater. The immersion heater has a power of 35 W. *Grade 4-5*

a) Calculate the energy transferred by the immersion heater when it is used for 600 s.
Use the equation:

$$\text{power} = \frac{\text{energy transferred}}{\text{time}}$$

Energy transferred = ... J
[3]

b) The student then uses the immersion heater to heat a second beaker of water.
The heater transfers 16 800 J of energy. Calculate the time that the heater was on for.

Time = ... s
[3]
[Total 6 marks]

Chapter P4 — Explaining Motion

Kinetic and Potential Energy Stores

1 A cyclist is travelling along a road at 5.0 m/s. The total energy in the kinetic energy stores of the cyclist and the bike is 1.1 kJ.

Calculate the total mass of the cyclist and bike.
Use the equation:
$$\text{kinetic energy} = 0.5 \times \text{mass} \times (\text{speed})^2$$

Mass = ... kg
[Total 4 marks]

2 A girl kicks a ball resting on the ground into the air.
The ball reaches a height of 2.0 m. The ball has a mass of 0.50 kg.
Gravitational field strength = 10 N/kg.

a) State the equation that links gravitational potential energy, mass, gravitational field strength and height.

....
[1]

b) Calculate the energy transferred to the ball's gravitational potential energy store.

Energy = ... J
[2]

c) The ball falls back down to the ground. All of the energy stored in the ball's gravitational potential energy store is transferred to its kinetic energy store.
Calculate the speed of the ball when it hits the ground.
Give your answer to 2 significant figures.

Speed = ... m/s
[3]
[Total 6 marks]

Exam Practice Tip

Be careful with equations involving squared values (^{2}), like the equation for kinetic energy above.
Make sure you remember to square the value (multiply it by itself) when you type it out in your calculator.

Chapter P4 — Explaining Motion

Describing Energy Transfers

1 Dorian is pushing a box along a flat, smooth surface. Dorian does 12.5 J of work on the box to increase its speed. There are no frictional forces acting on the box.

a) How much energy is transferred to the kinetic energy store of the box?

....
[1]

b) The box is moved onto a flat surface that is covered in carpet.
Dorian then does the same amount of work on the box to change its speed.
Which of the following statements are **true**? Place a tick (✓) in the box next to **two** statements.

More than 12.5 J is transferred to the kinetic energy store of the box. ☐

12.5 J of energy is transferred to the kinetic energy store of the box. ☐

Less than 12.5 J of energy is transferred to the kinetic energy store of the box. ☐

No friction acts between the box and the carpet. ☐

Friction acts between the box and the carpet. ☐

[2]
[Total 3 marks]

2 Vivienne is doing an experiment on a system. She measures the energy in the system before she does the experiment to be 1500 J. After the experiment, she measures the energy in the system again and finds it to be 900 J.

Vivienne makes the statement shown on the right.
Explain why Vivienne's statement is incorrect.

Vivienne
During the experiment, 700 J of energy was dissipated to useless energy stores.

....

....

....

....
[Total 2 marks]

3 A diver jumps from a diving board into a swimming pool.

Describe the energy transfers that occur as the diver falls towards the water.

....

....

....

....

....
[Total 4 marks]

Chapter P4 — Explaining Motion

Chapter P5 — Radioactive Materials

The History of the Atom

1 Which scientist suggested that electrons can only move around the nucleus at fixed distances? Place a tick (✓) in the box next to the correct answer.

Ernest Rutherford ☐

Niels Bohr ☐

Hans Geiger ☐

J.J. Thomson ☐

[Total 1 mark]

2 Our understanding of the structure of the atom has changed over time.

a) Dalton believed that atoms were tiny spheres which could not be broken up. Dalton's theory was shown to be incorrect by a discovery made by Thomson. State Thomson's discovery. Explain how it disproved Dalton's theory.

....

....

[2]

b) Thomson's discovery led to the development of the 'plum pudding' model of the atom. Describe the 'plum pudding' model.

....

....

[1]

[Total 3 marks]

3* Briefly describe the Rutherford-Geiger-Marsden alpha particle scattering experiment. Describe the observations made during the experiment. Explain what each observation suggested about the structure of a gold atom.

....

....

....

....

....

....

....

....

[Total 6 marks]

The Modern Model of the Atom

Warm-Up

Use the answers from the box below to fill in the table on the right.

0   −1   +1

Particle	Relative Charge
Proton	
Neutron	
Electron	

1 The sizes of atoms are often described using standard form.

a) What is the typical diameter of an atom?
Draw a circle around the correct answer.

1×10^{-20} m 1×10^{-15} m 1×10^{-10} m 1×10^{10} m

[1]

b) How does the diameter of the nucleus compare to the diameter of the atom?
Place a tick (✓) in the box next to the correct answer.

It is one tenth the diameter of the atom. ☐

It is one hundredth the diameter of the atom. ☐

It is one thousandth the diameter of the atom. ☐

It is one hundred-thousandth the diameter of the atom. ☐

[1]
[Total 2 marks]

2 Atoms are made up of protons, neutrons and electrons.

a) Describe how protons, neutrons and electrons are arranged in an atom.

....

....

....
[2]

b) Describe how mass and charge are distributed within an atom.

....

....

....
[2]
[Total 4 marks]

Exam Practice Tip

Remember, standard form is just a short-hand way of writing long numbers. If the power is positive, you're dealing with a big number. If the power is negative, it's a small number. E.g. $1.1 \times 10^5 = 110\ 000$ and $1.1 \times 10^{-5} = 0.000011$.

Chapter P5 — Radioactive Materials

Isotopes and Radioactive Decay

1 What is a beta particle identical to?
Place a tick (✓) in the box next to the correct answer.

Two protons and two neutrons ☐

A neutron ☐

An electron ☐

Electromagnetic radiation ☐

[Total 1 mark]

2 One isotope of sodium is $^{23}_{11}$Na.

a) State the mass number of this isotope.

....
[1]

b) Calculate the number of neutrons in the sodium nucleus.

Number of neutrons = ...
[1]

c) Which of the following is another isotope of sodium?
Place a tick (✓) in the box next to the correct answer.

$^{11}_{23}$Na ☐ $^{11}_{24}$Na ☐ $^{23}_{12}$Na ☐ $^{24}_{11}$Na ☐

[1]
[Total 3 marks]

3 Radiation sources A, B and C each emit a single type of radiation.
A detector was used to identify whether the radiation from each source was able to pass through paper or aluminium sheets. The results are shown below.

Name the type of radiation that source A emits. Explain your answer.

....

....

....
[Total 2 marks]

Chapter P5 — Radioactive Materials

Nuclear Equations

1 A strontium-90 nucleus decaying into yttrium-90 is shown below.

$$^{90}_{38}Sr \rightarrow ^{90}_{39}Y + ^{0}_{-1}e$$

Describe how the mass and charge of the nucleus change during the decay.

Nuclear mass: ....

Nuclear charge: ....

[Total 2 marks]

2 Nuclear equations show the products of radioactive decays.

a) Which of the following shows the symbol for two gamma rays produced by a decay?
Place a tick (✓) in the box next to the correct answer.

$^{0}_{0}\gamma$ ☐ $^{2}_{0}\gamma$ ☐ $^{0}_{2}\gamma$ ☐ $2^{0}_{0}\gamma$ ☐

[1]

b) Tellurium releases two beta particles as it decays into xenon.
Complete the following nuclear equation to show this.

$$^{128}_{52}Te \rightarrow ^{128}_{54}Xe + ...$$

[1]
[Total 2 marks]

3 A radium-226 nucleus decaying into radon is shown below.

$$^{226}_{88}Ra \rightarrow ^{a}_{b}Rn + ^{4}_{2}X$$

a) What particle is represented by **X** in this nuclear decay equation?

....

[1]

b) Calculate the values of a and b.

a = ...   b = ...

[2]

c) The radon (Rn) isotope then undergoes an alpha decay to form an isotope of polonium (Po). Write a balanced nuclear equation to show this.

....

[3]
[Total 6 marks]

Chapter P5 — Radioactive Materials

Activity and Half-life

Warm-Up

What is the activity of a source? Circle the correct answer.

| The number of protons in the source. | How far radiation from the source can travel before it's absorbed. | How many decays per second there are from the source. |

1 Radioactive decay is a random process. So half-life is used to find the activity of a source after a certain amount of time.

a) Explain what is meant by radioactive decay being 'random'.

....
....
[1]

b) Define the term 'half-life' in terms of activity.

....
....
[1]

c) The graph below shows how the activity of a radioactive sample changes over time. Using the graph, find the half-life of the sample.

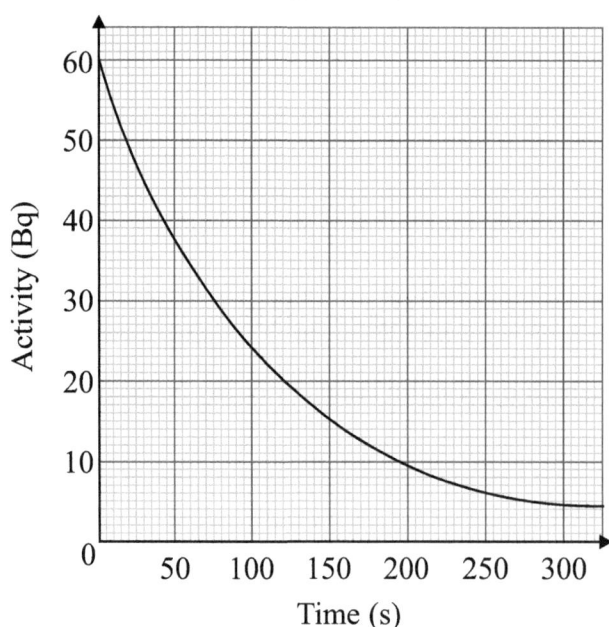

Half-life = ... s
[1]

[Total 3 marks]

Exam Practice Tip

When dealing with graphs, you can work out what each small square is worth on the scale by dividing the value of a big square by the number of small squares in it. For example, in the graph above, the big squares on the time scale are 50 s and there are 10 small squares inside each one. So, each small square on the time scale is worth (50 ÷ 10 =) 5 s.

Chapter P5 — Radioactive Materials

Dangers of Radioactivity

1 If a person's body is contaminated, they are exposed to ionising radiation. This can be dangerous.

a) Explain what is meant by 'contamination'.

....

....
[1]

b) Explain why exposure to ionising radiation can be dangerous.

....

....
[2]

[Total 3 marks]

2 A scientist writes out some safe handling instructions to be used in her lab while using radioactive isotopes.

> **Safety precautions for working with radioactive sources**
> - Always wear gloves when working with radioactive sources.
> - Keep sources as close to you as possible at all times.
> - Use tongs to handle any solid radioactive material.
> - Place sources in a lead lined box when not in use.

She has made **one** mistake.
Circle the incorrect statement. Explain why this statement is incorrect.

....

....
[Total 2 marks]

3 Explain why, for any source, contamination is more dangerous than irradiation.

....

....

....

....

....

....
[Total 4 marks]

More on the Dangers of Radioactivity

Warm-Up

Which of the following statements is **true**? Place a tick (✓) by the correct answer.

The higher the activity of a source, the safer it is to be around. ☐

The lower the activity of a source, the safer it is to be around. ☐

The activity of a source is not related to how safe it is. ☐

1   Ewan is comparing two radioactive sources, X and Y.
    Both sources emit the same type of radiation and have the same activity.
    Source X has a half-life of 24 hours and source Y has a half-life of 10 years.

Ewan makes the following statement:

Ewan
After any amount of time, source X will be safer to be around than source Y.

Is Ewan's statement true or false? Explain your answer.

....

....

....

....

....

[Total 3 marks]

2   Radium-226 is an alpha source. Radium-226 was used in clocks until the 1960s.

Should a clockmaker be more worried about contamination or irradiation when working on clocks made before 1960? Explain your answer.

....

....

....

....

....

....

[Total 3 marks]

Uses of Radiation

1 The table below outlines some properties of four radioactive sources. Which is the best source to use in a medical tracer?

	Type of radiation emitted	Half-life
A	Gamma	6 hours
B	Beta	500 years
C	Alpha	4 hours
D	Gamma	70 years

Answer ....
[Total 1 mark]

2 Nuclear radiation can be used to control or destroy cancerous tumours.

a) Use phrases from the box below to complete the passage about using nuclear radiation in medicine.

| gamma | can | outside | inside | beta | cannot |

.... sources are used to treat cancer from outside the body.

Alpha sources are used to treat cancer from .... the body.

The nuclear radiation emitted from both of these sources

.... destroy healthy cells.

[3]

b) Suggest why the half-life of the alpha source used to treat cancer must be short.

....

....

[1]
[Total 4 marks]

3 A patient is receiving treatment for a cancerous tumour. They are treated with an implant that contains a beta source.

a) Describe how the implant is used to treat the tumour.

....

....

....

[2]

b) The implant is removed after a few months. Suggest why.

....

....

[1]
[Total 3 marks]

Density

1 An irregularly-shaped stone has an unknown volume.

What equipment can be used for finding the volume of the stone?
Place a tick (✓) in the box next to the correct answer.

a thermometer ☐   a eureka can ☐   a balance ☐   a ruler ☐

[Total 1 mark]

PRACTICAL

2 Mallory has a balance, a measuring cylinder and some acid (a liquid). She wants to use the equipment to find the density of the acid.

Describe an experiment Mallory could do to calculate the density of the acid.

....

....

....

....

....

....

....

[Total 4 marks]

3 A block of tungsten has a mass of 7720 kg. Tungsten has a density of 19 300 kg/m^3.

a) State the equation for density.

....
[1]

b) Calculate the volume of the block of tungsten.

Volume = ... m^3
[3]

c) A 0.12 m^3 sample is cut from the block. Calculate the mass of the sample.
Give your answer to 2 significant figures.

Mass = ... kg
[4]

[Total 8 marks]

The Particle Model

Warm-Up

For each state of matter, draw the arrangement of the particles in the box provided. The first one has been done for you.

Solid | Liquid | Gas

1 Heating or cooling a substance can lead to a change of state.

a) Describe the following changes of state:

Melting: ....

Freezing: ....

Condensing: ....
[3]

b) A change of state is a physical change.
Use phrases from the box below to complete the passage.

| will | also called | will not | different to |

A physical change is .... a chemical change. If you reverse a

physical change, the substance .... get back its original properties.
[2]
[Total 5 marks]

2 A student fills a test tube with 30 g of water. He then heats the water so that it boils. The student's experiment is set up so that any water vapour produced is collected.

After a short time, the student stops boiling the water.
The mass of the water in the test tube is now 20 g.
State the mass of the water vapour collected by the student. Explain your answer.

....

....

....

....

....
[Total 2 marks]

More on the Particle Model

1 An ice cube is at its melting point. Sarah heats the ice cube so that it melts into water.

a) Which row of the table correctly describes what happens as the ice cube melts?

	Energy of the particles	Temperature of the ice cube and water
A	Increases	Increases
B	Decreases	Increases
C	Increases	Stays the same
D	Decreases	Stays the same

Your answer = ...
[1]

b) Once the ice cube has completely melted, Sarah continues heating the water that has been produced. The temperature of the water increases by 10 °C.
State how the average speed of the water particles changes during this time.

....
[1]
[Total 2 marks]

2 A tyre is pumped up to its maximum volume.

a) Describe how the motion of the air particles inside the tyre results in pressure on the tyre walls.

....
....
....
....
[3]

b) At its maximum volume, why would the tyre pressure be higher on a hot day compared to a cold day?

....
....
....
....
[3]
[Total 6 marks]

Exam Practice Tip

You need to be able to explain temperature changes or pressure on objects using the particle model.
Remember to talk about the energy of the particles, how close together they are and how quickly they're moving.

Specific Heat Capacity

1 Different substances have different specific heat capacities.

a) Explain what is meant by the specific heat capacity of a substance.

....

....
[1]

b) A block of nickel is heated. The total amount of energy transferred to the block is 8880 J. The mass of the block is 625 g. The temperature of the block increases by 32.0 °C. Calculate the specific heat capacity of nickel. Use an equation from the Equations List.

Specific heat capacity = ... J/kg°C
[4]

[Total 5 marks]

PRACTICAL

2* Eric carries out an experiment to find the specific heat capacity of aluminium. His set-up is shown below.

Describe a method Eric could use to safely find the specific heat capacity of aluminium. Your answer should include at least one safety precaution Eric should consider.

....

....

....

....

....

....

....

[Total 6 marks]

Chapter P6 — Matter — Models and Explanations

Specific Latent Heat

Warm-Up

Which of the following is the correct definition of specific latent heat? Tick **one** box.

The energy needed to raise the temperature of a substance by 1 °C. ☐

The maximum amount of energy an object can store before it melts. ☐

The energy needed to change the state of 1 kg of a substance without changing its temperature. ☐

The energy needed to change the state of 10 kg of a substance without changing its temperature. ☐

1 Explain the difference between specific heat capacity and specific latent heat. *(Grade 3-4)*

....

....

....

[Total 2 marks]

2 A student melts a sample of ice. *(Grade 4-5)*

a) 183.7 kJ of energy is transferred to the ice to completely melt it.
The temperature of the ice does not change during this time.
The specific latent heat of fusion for ice is 334 000 J/kg.
Calculate the mass of the sample. Use an equation from the Equations List.

Mass = ... kg
[4]

b) The ice is then heated until all of the sample boils and becomes a gas.
The specific latent heat of vaporisation of water is 2 260 000 J/kg.

Calculate the energy needed to completely boil the sample without changing its temperature.
Give your answer to 2 significant figures.

Energy = ... J
[3]

[Total 7 marks]

Exam Practice Tip

Watch out for units whenever you're doing calculations. The energies involved in changes of state are usually pretty large, so you may be given information in kJ instead of J. If you get an answer that seems too big or too small, check through your working to see if you've missed a unit conversion — it's an easy way to lose marks in the exam.

Chapter P6 — Matter — Models and Explanations

Heating and Doing Work

1 Patrick uses an immersion heater to heat a beaker of water. He measures the temperature of the water every 30 seconds. He stops his experiment before the water begins to boil.

a) Before the experiment, the water was at 20 °C.
After using the heater for 30 seconds, the temperature of the water was 35 °C.

What would you expect the temperature of the water to be after the heater was used for a further 30 seconds? Place a tick (✓) in the box next to the correct answer.

35 °C ☐ 50 °C ☐ 55 °C ☐ 70 °C ☐

[1]

b) Explain your answer to part a).

....
....
....
....
....

[3]
[Total 4 marks]

2 When a cyclist brakes, brake pads press against the bicycle's wheel. These pads apply a force to the bicycle wheel. This force does work. It slows down the bicycle and causes the brake pads to heat up.

a) A braking force of 90.0 N stops the bicycle in 8.0 m. Calculate the work done to stop the bicycle. Use the equation:

work done = force × distance

Work done = ... J
[2]

b) The total mass of the brake pads is 200 g.
The material the pads are made from has a specific heat capacity of 900 J/kg°C.
Calculate the temperature rise of the brake pads. Use an equation from the Equations List.
You can assume all of the energy transferred by the braking force was used to heat the pads.

Temperature rise = ... °C
[4]
[Total 6 marks]

Chapter P6 — Matter — Models and Explanations

Forces and Elasticity

1 The diagrams below show a spring before it is stretched, and the same spring while it is being stretched. *(Grade 1-3)*

Unstretched spring   Stretched spring

Which letter shows the extension of the spring? Draw a circle around the correct answer.

     A   B   C   D

[Total 1 mark]

2 A spring is stretched linearly by 0.08 m. The spring constant of the spring is 250 N/m. *(Grade 3-4)*

Calculate the force exerted by the spring.
Use the equation:

       force exerted by a spring = spring constant × extension

Force exerted = ... N
[Total 2 marks]

3 Janine pulls on either end of a spring. This causes the spring to stretch. *(Grade 3-4)*

a) Two forces are being applied to the spring to make it stretch.
Explain why more than one force is needed to make the spring stretch.

....

....
[1]

b) Janine pulls the spring so hard that it stops deforming elastically and begins to deform plastically. Describe the difference between elastic and plastic deformation.

....

....

....

....
[2]

[Total 3 marks]

Exam Practice Tip

Don't panic if you see a spring question that talks about compression instead of extension — you can still use the equation from question 2. Remember though, you can only use the equation for deformations that are <u>linear</u>.

Investigating Elasticity

PRACTICAL

1. Nick is investigating the relationship between the extension of a spring and the force acting on it. He hangs unit masses from the bottom of a spring to stretch it. He measures the extension of the spring for each force applied to the spring.

   The table below shows Nick's results.
   The graph is an incomplete force-extension graph of the results.

Force (N)	Extension (cm)
0.0	0.0
1.0	4.0
2.0	8.0
3.0	12.0
4.0	16.0
5.0	20.0

   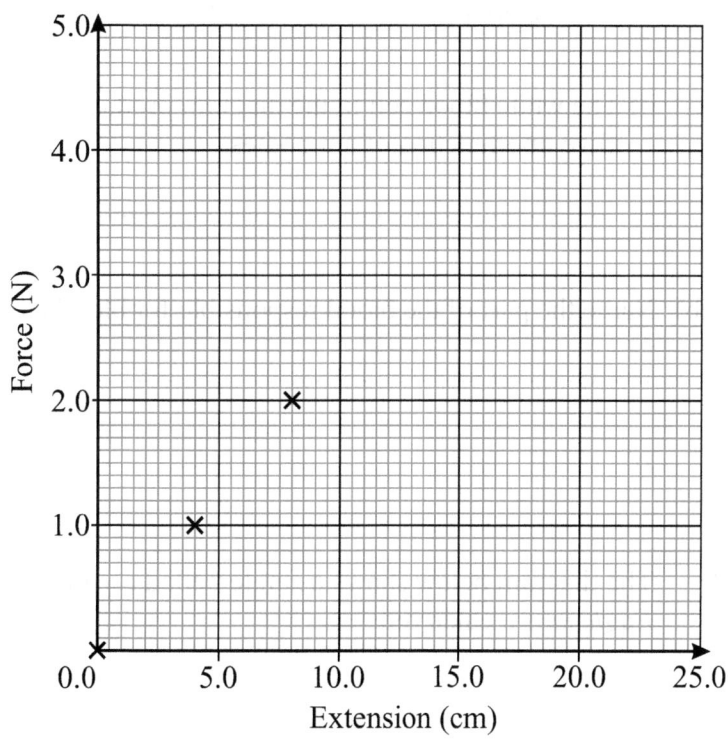

   a) Complete the graph above by plotting the missing data points and drawing a line of best fit.

   [3]

   b) Using the graph, calculate the work done to extend the spring by 10.0 cm.

   Work done = ... J

   [3]

   [Total 6 marks]

2. 0.18 J of work is done to stretch a spring. The spring is stretched elastically by 120 mm.

   Calculate the spring constant of the spring. Use an equation from the Equations List.

   Spring constant = ... N/m

   [Total 4 marks]

Chapter P6 — Matter — Models and Explanations

Biology Mixed Questions

1 The blood has several different parts.

a) The diagram on the right shows a white blood cell.

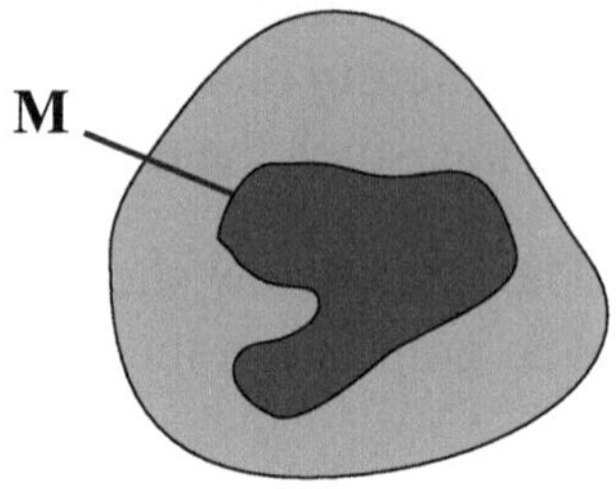

i) What is structure **M** on the diagram?
Place a tick (✓) in the box next to the correct answer.

cytoplasm ☐   nucleus ☐

cell membrane ☐   chloroplast ☐

[1]

ii) The white blood cell in the diagram produces antibodies.
Give **one** function of antibodies.

....
[1]

b) Name the part of the blood responsible for blood clotting.

....
[1]

[Total 3 marks]

2 The diagram below shows a single-celled organism called *Euglena*. *Euglena* is a eukaryote.

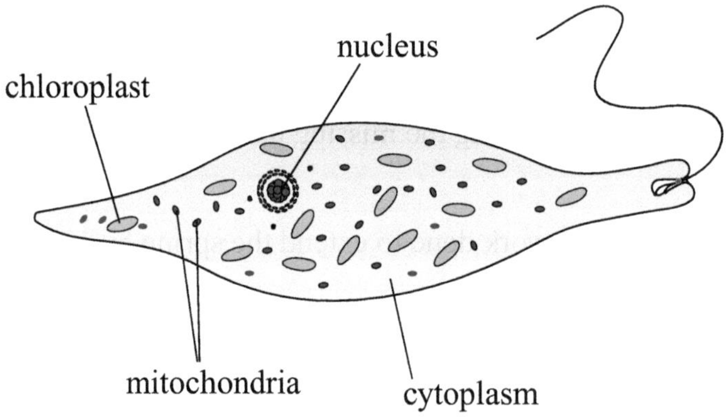

a) Give **one** piece of evidence from the diagram which shows that *Euglena* is a eukaryote and not a prokaryote.

....
[1]

b) Place a tick (✓) in the box that describes how *Euglena's* genetic material is stored.

as chromosomes in the nucleus ☐

as proteins in the nucleus ☐

as DNA in the cytoplasm ☐

as proteins in the cytoplasm ☐

[1]

[Total 2 marks]

3 In pea plants, seed shape is controlled by a single gene. *Grade 3-4*

The allele for round seed shape is R. The allele for wrinkled seed shape is r.
R is a dominant allele and r is recessive.

a) i) What is the **genotype** of a pea plant that is homozygous dominant for seed shape?
Place a tick (✓) in the box next to the correct answer.

RR ☐   rr ☐   wrinkled ☐   round ☐
[1]

ii) What is the **phenotype** of a pea plant that is homozygous dominant for seed shape?
Place a tick (✓) in the box next to the correct answer.

RR ☐   rr ☐   wrinkled ☐   round ☐
[1]

b) Two pea plants with a heterozygous genotype were crossed.
Complete the genetic diagram on the right to show the possible genotypes of the offspring.

	R	r
R		
r		

[1]
[Total 3 marks]

4 Aerobic respiration transfers energy from glucose. *Grade 3-4*

a) Complete the word equation for aerobic respiration.

glucose + ... → .... + water
[2]

Glucose is transported round the body in the blood.

b) i) The steps below describe what happens when the blood glucose level gets too high.
The steps are in the wrong order.
Write the letters (**A**, **B**, **C** or **D**) in the spaces provided to put the steps in the correct order.

A The pancreas releases insulin.

B Glucose is converted into glycogen for storage.

C Glucose moves into the liver and muscle cells.

D Receptors in the pancreas detect that the blood glucose level is too high.

....
[2]

ii) The blood glucose level is controlled in order to help maintain a constant internal environment. What name is given to the maintenance of a constant internal environment?

....
[1]
[Total 5 marks]

5   A plant cell with one of its subcellular structures magnified is shown below. The overall movement of four molecules into and out of the subcellular structure is also shown.

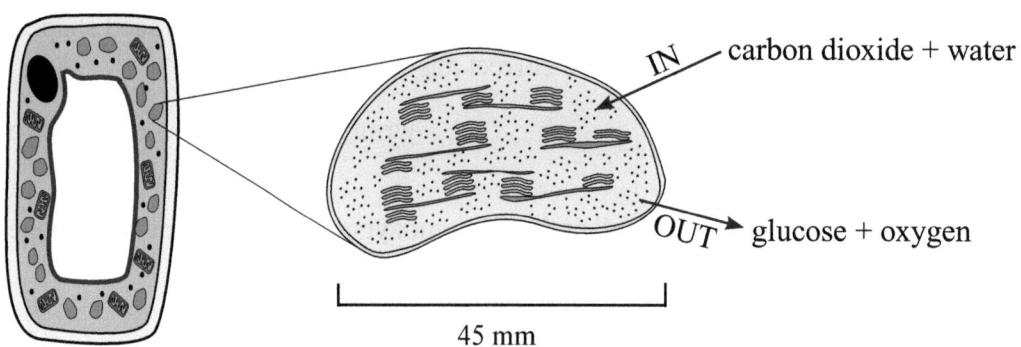

a) Look at the movements of carbon dioxide, water, glucose and oxygen shown above. What reaction do these movements suggest is taking place in the magnified subcellular structure?

....
[1]

b) What is the name of the magnified subcellular structure shown above?

....
[1]

c) The width of the subcellular structure when viewed using a microscope is 45 mm. What is the width of the magnified image in µm?
Place a tick (✓) in the box next to the correct answer.

45 000 µm ☐

0.045 µm ☐

4500 µm ☐

4.5 µm ☐

[1]

The cell shown above is from a leaf.

d) Describe how carbon dioxide enters a leaf.

....

....
[2]

e) What is the name of the process which transports water up a plant and into the leaves?

....
[1]

f) After glucose has been produced by a plant cell, some of it is converted to sucrose to be transported around the plant. What is the name of the transportation process?

....
[1]

[Total 7 marks]

6 Alcohol dehydrogenase enzymes break down alcohol in the body. *Grade 4-5*

a) Which of the following sentences about enzymes is correct?
Place a tick (✓) in the box next to the correct answer.

Enzymes speed up chemical reactions in living organisms. ☐

Enzymes are used up in chemical reactions. ☐

Enzymes are products of digestion. ☐

Enzymes are the building blocks of all living organisms. ☐

[1]

b) A scientist was investigating the effect of pH on the rate of activity of alcohol dehydrogenase. The graph below shows his results.

i) What is the optimum pH for the enzyme?

....
[1]

ii) Suggest and explain the effect an acid with a pH of 1 would have on the enzyme.

....

....

....
[3]

c) Which of the following statements about alcohol is correct?
Place a tick (✓) in the box next to the correct answer.

Alcohol is a risk factor for several communicable diseases. ☐

Alcohol is a risk factor for lung cancer. ☐

Alcohol can cause liver damage. ☐

Alcohol is not a risk factor for any disease. ☐

[1]

d) Alcohol can be produced by yeast cells when they respire.
What type of respiration is involved in the production of alcohol?

....
[1]

[Total 7 marks]

7 Part of a grassland food chain is shown below.

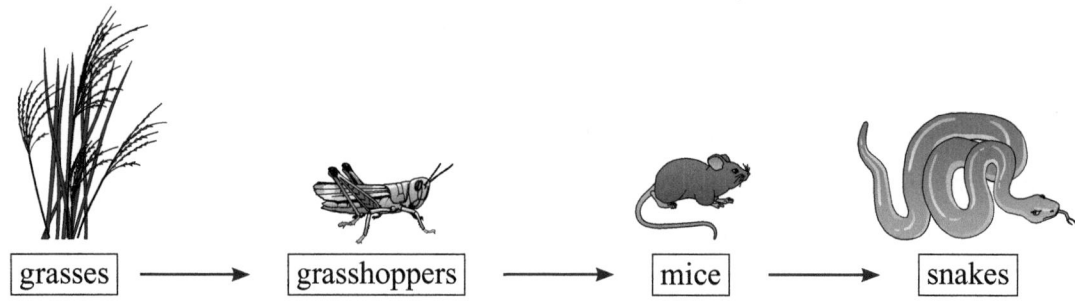

a) Grasses are the producer in this food chain.
What is meant by the term producer?

....

....
[1]

b) Suggest **one** biotic factor that may reduce the amount of grass in this food chain.

....
[1]

c) Mice are also eaten by owls.
What might happen to the population of **snakes** if owls were introduced into the ecosystem?
Give a reason for your answer.

....

....

....
[2]

d) A scientist is investigating the grassland ecosystem. Describe a method that the scientist could use to investigate whether the distribution of grasses changes across the ecosystem.

....

....

....
[3]

e) A farmer sprays the grass with herbicide.
Explain how the snake may end up consuming a toxic dose of the herbicide.

....

....

....
[2]

[Total 9 marks]

Mixed Questions

8 A student investigated whether light is needed for photosynthesis by green algae.

The student followed this method:
- Set up two boiling tubes as shown in the diagram on the right.
- Cover one of the boiling tubes with foil.
- Leave the tubes for several hours at room temperature with a constant light source.
- After this time, record the colour of the indicator solution.

a) The teacher suggested that the student should have also set up a boiling tube that only contained the indicator solution.

What would have been the purpose of this tube?

....
[1]

b) What was the purpose of the foil in this experiment?

....
[1]

The colour of the indicator solution is affected by the concentration of carbon dioxide in the boiling tube:

> If the carbon dioxide concentration **increases** from normal, the indicator turns **yellow**.
>
> If the carbon dioxide concentration **decreases** from normal, the indicator turns **purple**.

The colour of the indicator solution at the start and end of the experiment is shown in the table.

	Tube covered with foil?	Indicator colour at start	Indicator colour at end
Tube 1	yes	red	yellow
Tube 2	no	red	purple

c) The student concludes that:

"Photosynthesis occurred in Tube 2 but not in Tube 1."

Explain how the student can conclude this from the results.

....

....

....

....

....
[4]
[Total 6 marks]

Chemistry Mixed Questions

1   The nuclear symbol of an atom of a Group 1 element is shown below.

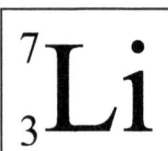

a) Write the name of the element that the nuclear symbol above represents.

   ....
   [1]

b) Name another element in the same group as the element shown above.

   ....
   [1]

c) Atoms contain protons, neutrons and electrons.

   i) How many protons does the atom shown above contain?

   ....
   [1]

   ii) Where in the atom would you find the neutrons?

   ....
   [1]

d) The element shown above is a metal. Which of the following diagrams shows the structure of a metal? Place a tick (✓) in the box next to the correct answer.

   [1]

e) The element Li reacts with water. One of the products of this reaction is a gas.
   When a lit splint is placed in the gas, a squeaky pop is heard.
   What is the name of the gas produced? Place a tick (✓) in the box next to the correct answer.

   carbon dioxide ☐

   chlorine ☐

   oxygen ☐

   hydrogen ☐

   [1]

   [Total 6 marks]

2 Harriet is making a salt by reacting sulfuric acid with potassium hydroxide. *(Grade 1-3)*

a) Place a tick (✓) in the box next to the salt that is formed in this reaction.

potassium chloride ☐

potassium sulfate ☐

potassium nitrate ☐

potassium carbonate ☐

[1]

b) The salt that forms is in solution. What state symbol would it have in a symbol equation?

....
[1]

c) The salt solution that forms is neutral. Give the pH of the salt solution.

....
[1]

[Total 3 marks]

3 Sulfur dioxide (SO_2) is a pollutant that causes acid rain when it mixes with clouds. *(Grade 3-4)*

a) Calculate the relative formula mass, M_r, of sulfur dioxide.
Relative atomic masses (A_r): S = 32.1, O = 16.0

Relative formula mass = ...
[1]

b) The melting point of sulfur dioxide is –73 °C. The boiling point of sulfur dioxide is –10 °C.
Give the physical state of sulfur dioxide when the temperature is –86 °C.

....
[1]

c) i) Sulfur dioxide reacts with oxygen gas to form sulfur trioxide (SO_3).
The symbol equation for this reaction is shown below. Balance the equation.

$$..........SO_{2(g)} + O_{2(g)} \rightleftharpoons ....SO_{3(g)}$$

[1]

ii) Which of the following describes the type of reaction shown in part c) i)?
Draw a circle around the correct answer.

displacement   neutralisation   reversible   precipitation

[1]

[Total 4 marks]

4 Hydrochloric acid (HCl) and sodium hydroxide (NaOH) react in a neutralisation reaction.

a) A student carries out a titration to find the volume of hydrochloric acid needed to neutralise 25 cm³ of sodium hydroxide. She does the experiment three times. Her results are shown below.

Repeat	1	2	3
Volume (cm³)	35.60	35.65	35.65

Calculate the mean volume of hydrochloric acid needed to neutralise the sodium hydroxide.

mean = ... cm³
[2]

b) The student measures the pH of the sodium hydroxide at the start of the experiment.
During the experiment, she measures the pH of the solution at regular intervals.
She measures the pH again at the end of the reaction.

Describe how the pH of the reaction mixture would change over the course of the experiment.

....
....
....
....
[3]

c) The products of the reaction between hydrochloric acid and sodium hydroxide are sodium chloride and water. Write a balanced symbol equation for this reaction.

....
[2]

d) The sodium chloride dissolves in the water, forming an aqueous solution.

i) Suggest a technique that the student could use to produce a pure sample of solid sodium chloride from this solution.

....
[1]

ii) Suggest a technique that she could use to produce a pure sample of water from this solution.

....
[1]

e) Sodium chloride is an ionic compound formed from a Group 1 metal and a Group 7 element. What is the charge on the sodium ion in sodium chloride?

....
[1]

[Total 10 marks]

5 Ezra is using a paper chromatography experiment to analyse a sample.
The chromatogram produced by the experiment is shown below.

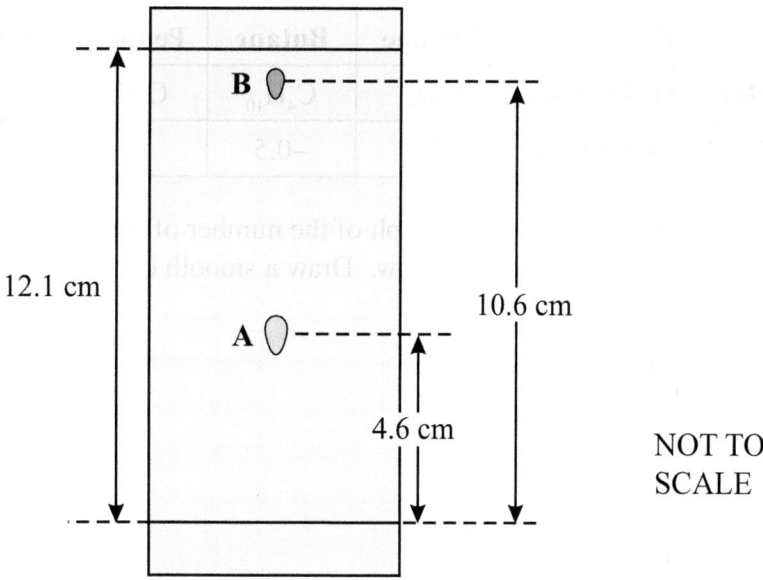

a) Ezra thinks that the sample is a pure substance. Is Ezra correct? Explain your answer.

....

....
[2]

b) Use the chromatogram shown above to calculate the Rf values for spots **A** and **B**.
Give both Rf values to 2 significant figures.

$$Rf = \frac{\text{distance travelled by solute}}{\text{distance travelled by solvent}}$$

Rf of **A** = ...

Rf of **B** = ...
[2]

c) The sample contains an ionic compound.
The diagram below shows the structure of a solid ionic compound.

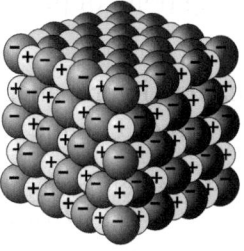

Give **one advantage** and **one disadvantage** of using this type of diagram to show ionic compounds.

Advantage: ....

Disadvantage: ....
[2]
[Total 6 marks]

Mixed Questions

6 Alkanes are hydrocarbon compounds found in crude oil. The table below shows how the boiling points of the alkanes change as the molecules get bigger.

Alkane	Propane	Butane	Pentane	Hexane	Heptane
Molecular formula	C_3H_8	C_4H_{10}	C_5H_{12}	C_6H_{14}	C_7H_{16}
Boiling point (°C)	−42	−0.5		69	98

a) Using the data in the table, plot a graph of the number of carbon atoms in an alkane molecule against boiling point on the axes below. Draw a smooth curve through the points that you plot.

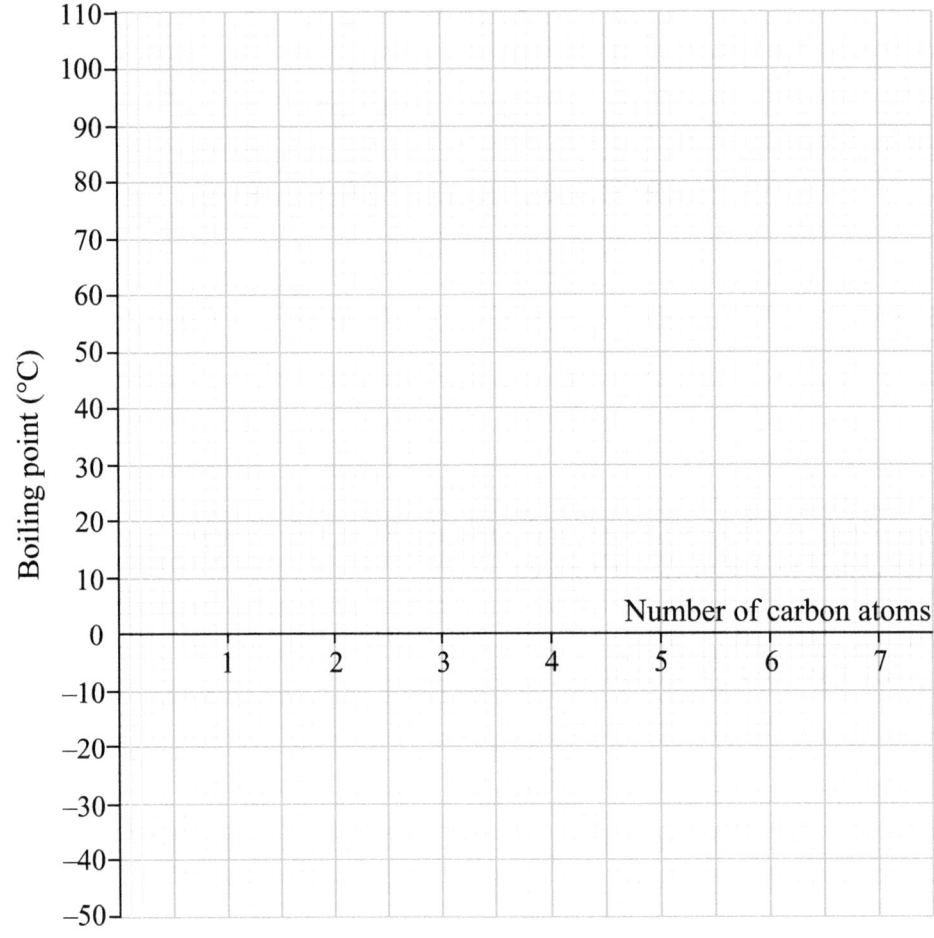

[2]

b) Use your graph to estimate the boiling point of pentane. .... °C

[1]

c) Calculate the percentage mass of carbon in propane, C_3H_8.
Give your answer to 3 significant figures. Use the equation:

Percentage mass of element in a compound = $\dfrac{A_r \text{ of element} \times \text{number of atoms of element}}{M_r \text{ of compound}} \times 100$

(A_r of carbon = 12.0, A_r of hydrogen = 1.0)

percentage mass = ... %

[3]

[Total 6 marks]

7 Zinc oxide is a compound which has many important uses. *(Grade 4-5)*

   a) Zinc oxide can be used as a catalyst in the chemical industry.
      How does a catalyst increase the rate of a reaction?

      ....

      ....
      [2]

   b) Some sunscreens contain nanoparticles of zinc oxide.
      Suggest **two** potential risks of using nanoparticles in sunscreens.

      1. ....

      ....

      2. ....

      ....
      [2]

   c) Zinc oxide is also used in the ceramic industry. Give **two** properties of ceramics.

      1. ....

      2. ....
      [2]
      [Total 6 marks]

8 A student reacts some dilute potassium hydroxide with some dilute sulfuric acid. *(Grade 4-5)*
   During the experiment, the temperature changes from 22 °C to 31 °C.

   a) Is this reaction endothermic or exothermic? Explain your answer.

      ....
      [1]

   b) Will the energy of the products be higher or lower than the energy of the reactants?

      ....
      [1]

   c) The student repeated the reaction using a more concentrated solution of sulfuric acid.
      State how increasing the concentration of the acid will affect the rate of the reaction.
      Explain your answer in terms of the collisions between the reacting particles.

      ....

      ....

      ....

      ....
      [3]
      [Total 5 marks]

9 Aluminium and iron can be obtained by extracting them from their ores. Both metals can also be obtained from recycling aluminium and iron items.

Material	Extraction process	Energy saved by recycling
Aluminium	Electrolysis	Around 95%
Iron	Reduction with carbon	Around 60%

a) This is the balanced symbol equation for the extraction of iron from iron oxide:

$$2Fe_2O_3 + 3C \rightarrow 4Fe + 3CO_2$$

Give the formula of the substance that is reduced during this reaction. Explain how you can tell.

....
[2]

b) The table shows that energy is saved when aluminium and iron are obtained from recycling rather than being extracted from their ores. Suggest **two** other advantages of recycling materials.

1. ....

2. ....
[2]
[Total 4 marks]

10 The table below shows some of the properties of diamond and graphite.

	Hardness	Melting point	Conducts electricity?
Diamond	Hard	High	No
Graphite	Soft	High	Yes

a)* Explain how the structure and bonding of diamond and graphite give them these properties. Your answer should include details of how the atoms are arranged and held together.

....

....

....

....

....

....

....

....
[6]

b) Diamond and graphite are both forms of carbon. What is the electronic structure of carbon?

....
[1]
[Total 7 marks]

Physics Mixed Questions

1 Electrical power is transferred from power stations around the UK by the national grid. *Grade 1-3*

a) What is a step-up transformer used for in the national grid?

....

....

[1]

Electricity can be generated from non-renewable and renewable resources.

b) Give **one** example of a non-renewable energy resource.

....

[1]

c) i) Give **one** reason why many people think more electricity should be generated by renewable energy resources.

....

[1]

ii) Give **one** reason why so much of the world's electricity is still generated by non-renewables.

....

[1]

[Total 4 marks]

2 The image on the right is a displacement-distance graph for a microwave. *Grade 1-3*

a) What is the amplitude of the wave?
Place a tick (✓) in the box next to the correct answer.

   3 cm ☐   2 cm ☐   6 cm ☐   18 cm ☐

[1]

b) Microwaves are electromagnetic waves. All electromagnetic waves are transverse waves. State what it means when a wave is said to be transverse.

....

....

[1]

c) State **one** use of microwaves.

....

[1]

[Total 3 marks]

3 Loreen is investigating the relationship between mass and weight.

a) Use words from the box below to complete the passage.

| gravitational | kilograms | electrostatic | newtons | magnetic | newton metres |

Weight is a force caused by the .... fields around objects interacting.

It is measured in ....

[2]

b) Loreen uses a spring balance to measure the weight of her full pencil case.
The weight of the pencil case is 6.0 N.
It causes the spring in the spring balance to extend by 0.03 m.

i) State the energy store of the spring that energy is being transferred to when it extends.

....

[1]

ii) Calculate the spring constant of the spring.
Use the equation:

force exerted on a spring = extension × spring constant

Spring constant = ... N/m

[3]

c) Loreen makes the following statement:

Loreen
My pencil case would have the same weight on a planet with a lower gravitational field strength.

Is she correct? Explain your answer.

....

....

....

[2]

d) Loreen removes items from her pencil case until the mass of the pencil case has halved.
State the new weight of the pencil case.

Weight = ... N

[1]

[Total 9 marks]

4 Anya is investigating light. She uses a ray box to direct a thin beam of light at a flat surface made from an unknown material. *(Grade 3-4)*

a) State the **three** different things which can happen to a light wave when it reaches a boundary between two materials.

1. ....

2. ....

3. ....
[3]

b) The beam of light hits the surface at 25° to the normal and reflects off the surface. State the angle of reflection of the beam.

Angle of reflection = ... °
[1]

c) The ray box contains a circuit consisting of a battery and a filament lamp. The current through the filament lamp while the ray box is in use is 3.5 A. The ray box is used for 240 s. Calculate the total charge that passes through the filament lamp while the ray box is in use.

Charge = ... C
[3]
[Total 7 marks]

5 The table on the right contains information about four atoms. *(Grade 4-5)*

a) State which two atoms in the table are isotopes of the same element. Explain your answer.

	Mass number	Atomic number
Atom A	127	53
Atom B	135	53
Atom C	135	55
Atom D	137	56

....

....

....
[2]

b) Atom D emits a gamma ray. The gamma ray travels at a speed of 3.0×10^8 m/s and has a frequency of 1.5×10^{20} Hz. Calculate the wavelength of the gamma ray.

Wavelength = ... m
[4]

c) Give **one** risk associated with exposure to gamma rays.

....
[1]
[Total 7 marks]

Mixed Questions

6 Heater A and Heater B are two electric heaters. It takes 340 s for Heater A to heat 0.50 kg of water from 25 °C to 45 °C.

a) Calculate the energy transferred to the thermal energy store of the water.
The specific heat capacity of water is 4200 J/kg °C. Use an equation from the Equations List.

Change in thermal energy = ... J
[3]

b) It takes Heater B 170 s to heat 0.50 kg of water from 25 °C to 45 °C. You can assume both heaters are 100% efficient. You can also assume all the energy is transferred to the water.

State which of the two heaters has the higher power rating. Explain your answer.

....

....

....
[3]

[Total 6 marks]

7 Sam is using a radiation detector to investigate a radioactive source, A.

a) Sam puts source A in a sealed box lined with a thin layer of lead. When he places the radiation detector near the box, the detector still detects radiation from the source.
Sam and his friend Maxine both suggest what type of radiation is being detected from source A:

Sam
The detector is detecting gamma rays from source A.

Maxine
The detector is detecting alpha particles from source A.

State whether Sam or Maxine is correct. Explain your answer.

....

....

....
[2]

b) Maxine is investigating the radiation emitted by a sample of nickel-63.
Maxine writes the equation below for nickel-63 emitting a beta particle.

$$^{63}_{28}\text{Ni} \rightarrow ^{A}_{29}\text{Cu} + ^{B}_{-1}e$$

Determine the values of A and B.

A = ...

B = ...
[2]

[Total 4 marks]

Mixed Questions

8 A student creates the circuit shown on the right. Three points are labelled on the circuit as A, B and C.   *Grade 4-5*

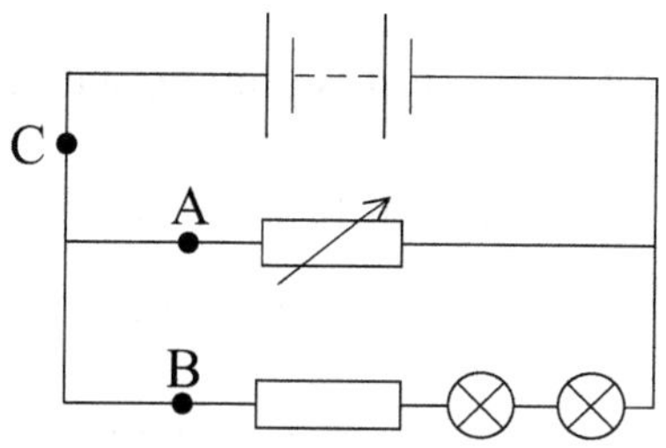

a) Name **one** component that is in parallel with the filament bulbs.

....
[1]

b) i) The current at Point A is 5.0 A. The current at Point B is 2.0 A. Calculate the current at Point C.

Current at Point C = ... A
[1]

ii) The battery has a potential difference of 9.0 V. Calculate the power of the variable resistor. Use the equation:

power = potential difference × current

Power = ... W
[2]

c) The student removes the variable resistor from the circuit. Explain the effect this has on the brightness of the bulbs.

....
....
....
[2]
[Total 6 marks]

9 A 0.455 kg lump of butter has a volume of 5.00×10^{-4} m^3.   *Grade 4-5*

a) Calculate the density of the butter.

Density = ... kg/m^3
[3]

b) The butter is placed in a pan and heated on an electric hob. The butter begins to melt. Describe how the density of the butter changes as it melts. You should refer to the arrangement of particles in your answer.

....
....
....
....
[4]
[Total 7 marks]

10   A child is playing with a remote-controlled toy car.

   a) The car has a mass of 1.0 kg. The car is travelling at 6.0 m/s.

      i) Give the equation that links kinetic energy, mass and speed.

      ....
      [1]

      ii) Calculate the amount of energy in the car's kinetic energy store.

      Energy = ... J
      [2]

   b) The car is powered by an electric motor.
      The total energy transferred to the motor in 2 minutes is 0.75 kJ.

      i) Give the equation that links energy transferred, charge and potential difference.

      ....
      [1]

      ii) The potential difference across the electric motor is 2.5 V.
          Calculate the total charge that passes through the motor during these 2 minutes.

      Charge = ... C
      [4]

   c) The car has a bar magnet attached to the back of it. The child places a toy trailer next to the magnet.
      This is shown in the diagram below. The trailer is made from a material that contains iron.

      When the car moves, the trailer moves with the car. Explain why.

      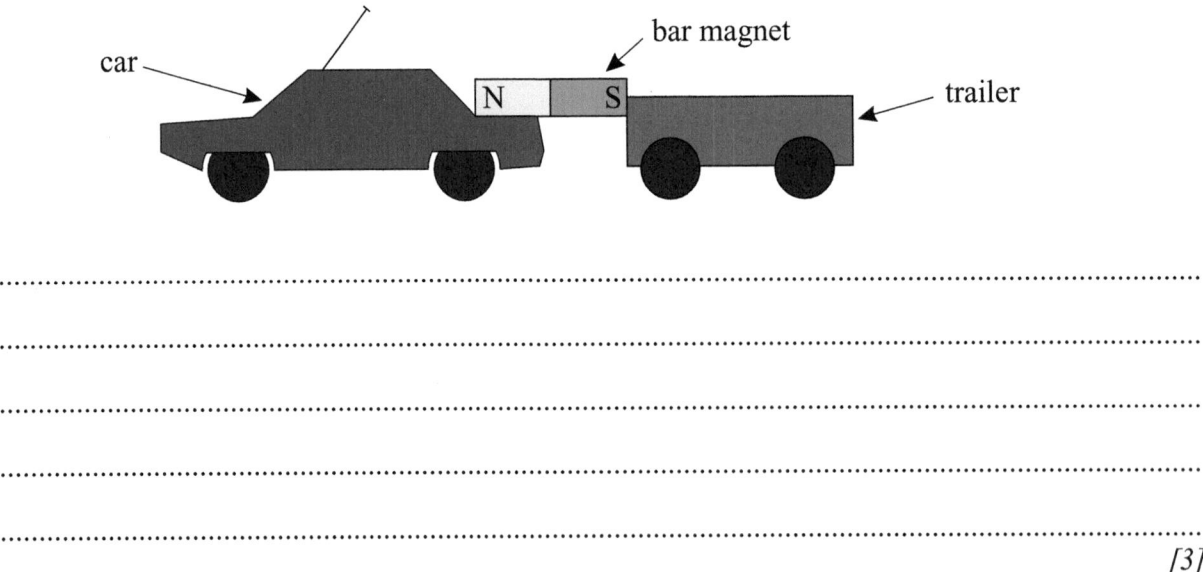

      ....
      ....
      ....
      ....
      ....
      [3]
      [Total 11 marks]